BRI

ACCESS
GERMAN

ACCESS
GERMAN

Henriette Harnisch

Series editor: **Jane Wightwick**

Hodder & Stoughton
A MEMBER OF THE HODDER HEADLINE GROUP

Orders: please contact Bookpoint Ltd, 130 Milton Park, Abingdon, Oxon OX14 4SB.
Telephone: (44) 01235 827720. Fax: (44) 01235 400454. Lines are open from 9.00–6.00, Monday
to Saturday, with a 24-hour message answering service. You can also order through our website:
www.hodderheadline.co.uk

British Library Cataloguing in Publication Data
A catalogue record for this title is available from the British Library

ISBN 0 340 849150

First Published 2003
Impression number   10 9 8 7 6 5 4 3 2 1
Year   2007 2006 2005 2004 2003

Copyright © 2003 Henriette Harnisch

Typeset and illustrated by Hardlines Ltd, Charlbury, Oxford
Printed in Italy for Hodder & Stoughton Educational, a division of Hodder Headline Plc, 338
Euston Road, London NW1 3BH

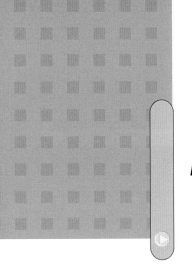

ACKNOWLEDGEMENTS

The authors and publishers would like to thank the following for use of their material in this volume:

5310.com for *Ferien Kriterien* web page p80; www.aachen.de for their web page p1; Restaurant Adlon Stube, Berlin for web listing on p76; Restaurant Amadeus, Hamburg for web listing p76; Restaurant Alcatraz III, Berlin for web listing p76; Hotel Asam, Munich for their web page p48; Arbeitsamt online for their web page *Arbeiten im Ausland* p21; www.tdaudiopromotion.de for web page *Lassen Sie was von sich hören* packet p166; Bayer Vital for Aspirin packet p105; Berliner Verkehrsbetriebe for tariff p59; Restaurant Borchardt for web listing p76; www.brueckenbauer.ch for web page recipe p72; Restaurant Come Prima for web listing p76; Eden for Cevita advert p100; Café Einstein, Berlin for web listing p76; Google.de for web page p168; HB Verlag, Hamburg for article *Mecklenburg-Vorpommerns Inselwelt* on p87; Herren & Co for Visitenkarten on p11; www.Hobbythek.de for web page *Zeigt her eure Füße* on p38; www.jobpilot.de for web page *Finden Sie den Job Ihres Lebens* p119; www.job-suche.de for web page *Jobscout 24* p138; Galeria Kaufhof for web shopping pages p43; Wolfgang Kurtz/kpunkt.com for Nature Pages p98; Lichtwer Pharma AG for Kwai packet p105; managerSeminare/ebay for article *Die Bausteine des Lebens* p142; www.sintcon.de for web page p157; www.stadtplandienst.de for map of Berlin centre p48; www.stepstone.de for web page *Jobsuche* p138; Das Telefonbuch for web listings on p25; Anke Thede for *Suchen* web page p170; www.wdr.de for programme pages p40; working@office – Das Magazin für die Frau im Büro, Gabler Verlag, Wiesbaden, vol. 11/2001 p7, URL http://www.workingoffice.de for article p160; yahoo.com/de for jobs web page p2.

Every effort has been made to trace and acknowledge ownership of copyright. The publishers will be glad to make suitable arrangements with any copyright holders whom it has not been possible to contact.

Photo acknowledgements

AKG p127 (top), p129 (bottom), p130 (bottom). S. Baldwin p39, p43. Corbis p64 (nos. 1 & 6), p90, p130 (top, centre), p154. Ronald Grant p6 (top left). Das Fotoarchiv p18 (top centre & right, bottom row), p31, p34 (top & bottom), p54 (nos. 1, 5 & 7), p55, p58, p83, p88 (centre), p122 (centre), p127 (bottom), p133 (top left, bottom right), p147. I. Mungall p88 (right). Rex Features Ltd p6 (top right, bottom left & right), p18 (top left). Still Pictures p54 (no. 3), p64 (nos. 2, 3, 4 & 5). C. Weiss p133 (top right, bottom left).

Cover illustration: © 2002 Corbis.

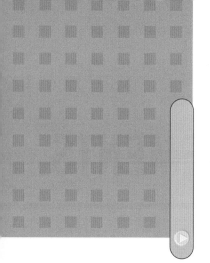

INTRODUCTION

Access German is a refreshing, modern introduction to the German language, culture and people. It is specially designed for adults of all ages who are just starting out learning German or who are returning after a long gap.

The course is ideal for use in classes but will also help develop strategies for independent learning. In the coursebook, teachers and learners will find an extended range of activities covering all four skills as well as ideas for group activities.

A further range of ideas, activities, tips and advice is available on our website, www.accesslanguages.com. You don't have to use the site to benefit from the course but, according to your particular needs or interests, you will find a great deal of extra practice, information and links to useful German sites. For more depth in a particular language structure, for example, we have included additional interactive activities and we've even included advice and links for the major examinations and qualifications.

Access German offers a fun and friendly approach to the German language as it is spoken in Germany and other German-speaking countries today. It will enable you to deal with everyday situations, covering practical topics such as travel, shopping, making a complaint at a hotel or eating in a restaurant and many of the activities are based on genuine German websites. The course is also ideal for those who wish to study German for business purposes and will provide learners with a sound basis of vocabulary and grammar structures.

The coursebook is divided into 10 carefully graded units. At the beginning of each, the content and objectives are clearly identified and you can check your progress at various points throughout the unit. Each unit starts with a number of activities relating to the previous one so you can revise topics already covered, giving you the confidence to move on to new areas.

The units offer a wide range of activities which will quickly enable you to start reading and writing contemporary German, and the listening exercises featuring authentic German-speakers are integral to the course.

Each unit consists of:

- a checklist of topics covered in the unit

- revision activities (Wissen Sie noch?): these give you the chance to revise important points covered in the previous unit

- listening activities: authentic conversations, passages and exercises to increase your listening skills and to help you acquire confidence

- speaking activities

- reading activities: authentic documents and exercises to extend your vocabulary and comprehension

- writing activities: practical and authentic forms to complete, grammar activities and letter-writing to consolidate key points and to reinforce confidence when travelling to a German-speaking country

- exercises and games to work on with a partner

- exercises and games to work on with a group in order to practise the language through various practical situations

- games to be played with a partner or in a group

- **LANGUAGE FOCUS** Language Focus panels: these offer brief and concise structural and grammatical summaries with related activities

- **LEARNING TIP:** Learning Tip: containing useful linguistic and cultural information

- **READY TO MOVE ON?** Ready to move on: frequent reviews enabling you to check your progress and to feel confident in what you have learnt

- **GLOSSARY** : German-English glossaries containing vocabulary used in the unit

- **LOOKING FORWARD** : preparation and dictionary skills ready for the next unit

- website: links to our dedicated website www.accesslanguages.com containing extra activities to practise key points, useful links to German sites and advice on further study and qualifications

Answers to the exercises and recording transcripts are available in a separate Support Booklet and we strongly recommend that you obtain the **Access German Support Book and Cassette Pack**, which will enable you to develop your listening skills and get used to hearing the German language as it is spoken now.

We hope that working through this course will be an enjoyable experience and that you will find this new approach to language learning fun!

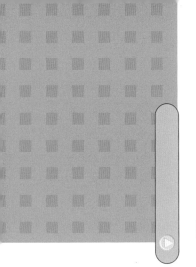

CONTENTS

UNIT 1
Willkommen

By the end of this unit you will be able to:

- Say hello and introduce yourself
- Attract somebody's attention
- Understand different ways of greeting and react accordingly
- Understand some simple signs and questions
- Talk about where you live
- Talk about what your hobbies are
- Say the numbers up to 10
- Say the German alphabet

We suggest that you come back to this checklist as you progress through the unit. You can then judge how you are getting on.

Recognising words or phrases in German is not always as difficult as it seems.

The Internet age has hugely accelerated the immigration of English and American words into the German language. Whether you like it or not, and some Germans are not too happy about it, it does mean that to begin with, you only need a few words to find your way around. Prove this to yourself by listening to a natural German dialogue straight away.

1 Hören Sie mal!

A Listen to the dialogue and tick the information asked for. Don't worry at this stage about understanding every word. Just see if you can get the gist.

- Profession
- Address
- Telephone number
- Name
- Marital status

B Listen to the same dialogue again and put the words of the question below in the right order.

| NAME | WIE | IHR | IST | ? |

Did you pick out the answer to the question in the dialogue?

C Now work in pairs and ask your partner what his or her name is. When replying, say:

Mein Name ist ... or **Ich heiße ...**

2 Wie heißen Sie?

Listen to the dialogue and fill in the gaps with the following words:

(Wie)   (Name)   (Abend)   (Ich)   (Guten)

Dialogue

Guten (_____).

Mein (_____) ist Helmut Krause.

(_____) ist Ihr Name?

(_____) heiße Karin Schmidt.

Angenehm.

(_____) Abend.

LEARNING TIP:

If you did not catch an answer, or someone is speaking too fast, you can ask them to repeat what they said by using: **Wie, bitte?** (*Pardon?*), **Noch einmal, bitte** (literally: *Again, please.*) or **Langsamer, bitte** (*Slower, please*).

You may have heard people greeting each other with the phrases **Guten Tag** and **Guten Abend**. As a rule of thumb, you can assume that **Guten Tag** is used during office hours, and **Guten Abend** after office hours. First thing in the morning you will also hear **Guten Morgen**.
Auf Wiedersehen or **Tschüs** are used to say 'goodbye', but nowadays you will hear people say **Hi!** and **Ciao!** for 'hello' and 'goodbye' just as often.

Willkommen

UNIT 1

3

3 Ich heiße Adam

Mix-and-match game. Your teacher will give you a card with a name on it. Go round the class and find the person who forms the other half of your pair (for example, Adam – Eve). Here are some words to help you:

- **Guten Tag.**
- **Guten Tag.**
- **Wie ist Ihr Name?** or **Wie heißen Sie?**
- **Mein Name ist...** or **Ich heiße...**
- **Danke.**
- **Bitte.**
- **Tschüs.**
- **Auf Wiedersehen.**

4 Formulare, Formulare

  Look at the personal details form on the next page.

Work with a partner for this exercise. Ask your partner for the information needed to fill in the blanks. When you have finished, swap roles. If you have forgotten any of the vocabulary, check in the vocabulary section for this unit.

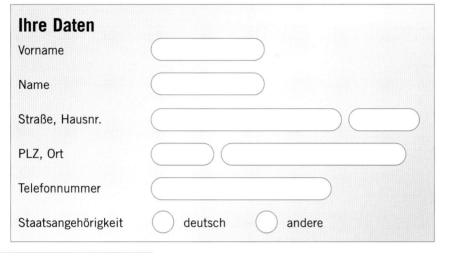

Ihre Daten

Vorname	
Name	
Straße, Hausnr.	
PLZ, Ort	
Telefonnummer	
Staatsangehörigkeit	○ deutsch ○ andere

LANGUAGE FOCUS

Before you start, check again how the question was asked in the previous exercise:

Wie ist Ihr Name?

As you can see, the word order is very similar to the English question, starting with a question word:

question word	verb	noun	question mark
Wie	ist	Ihr Name	?

These are the items of information you are asking for:
- der Vorname
- der Name
- die Straße
- die Hausnummer
- die Postleitzahl
- der Ort

(**der** Name) ⟶ (**Ihr** Name)

(**die** Straße) ⟶ (**Ihre** Straße)

Mein/meine (*my*) and **Ihr/Ihre** (*your*) are pronouns that indicate possession.

Willkommen UNIT 1

READY TO MOVE ON?

✓

Check that you can...

- ask and answer questions about your name in two different ways
- say 'please' and 'thank you'
- greet someone at different times of the day
- say goodbye.

5 Wer ist das?

A 🎲 ⊙ Study the pictures below, read the information in the boxes, then match the photos with the text. Remember to read for the general gist – don't expect to understand every word.

1 ▷ Sie ist eine berühmte amerikanische Schauspielerin und Sängerin. Sie ist eine Pop-Ikone, und Kritiker nennen sie ein Chamäleon. Ihr Mann ist Filmregisseur und kommt aus England.

2 ▷ Er ist der Premierminister von England. Seine Frau heißt Cherie. Er hat vier Kinder. Er wohnt in Number 10 Downing Street.

3 ▷ Er ist ein berühmter Schauspieler. Er kommt aus Schottland. Die Frauen lieben ihn!

4 ▷ Der Mann ist ein Pop-Sänger. Er ist ein Star in der ganzen Welt. Seine Fans sind vor allem junge Mädchen.

a

b

c

d

B 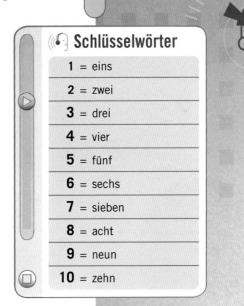 Now look at the sentences below. Fill in the missing words. The answers are in the texts on the previous page!

1 • Er ⬭⬭⬭⬭⬭⬭⬭ vier Kinder.

2 • Sie ⬭⬭⬭⬭⬭⬭⬭ Sängerin.1

3 • Er ⬭⬭⬭⬭⬭⬭⬭ aus Schottland.

4 • Die Frauen ⬭⬭⬭⬭⬭⬭⬭ ihn.

5 • Sie ⬭⬭⬭⬭⬭⬭⬭ aus Amerika.

6 • Er ⬭⬭⬭⬭⬭⬭⬭ in Number 10 Downing Street.

7 • Er ⬭⬭⬭⬭⬭⬭⬭ ein Pop-Star.

8 • Seine Frau ⬭⬭⬭⬭⬭⬭⬭ Cherie.

Can you guess what each sentence means?

You'll find an activity to help you remember the numbers on www.accesslanguages.com

Schlüsselwörter

1	=	eins
2	=	zwei
3	=	drei
4	=	vier
5	=	fünf
6	=	sechs
7	=	sieben
8	=	acht
9	=	neun
10	=	zehn

6 Arbeit mit Zahlen

In this puzzle, we have hidden the numbers one to ten. Can you find them?

A	S	S	I	E	B	E	N	W	B	P	Z	I	P
C	V	E	Ä	D	E	Ä	U	E	A	O	W	E	O
H	Ü	R	D	E	D	S	R	S	R	R	E	N	D
T	K	T	E	R	R	S	T	T	B	T	I	F	E
Y	O	Y	T	S	E	C	H	S	A	T	O	E	I
T	F	F	O	T	I	U	Ö	Z	E	H	N	E	N
R	B	Ü	L	U	D	P	R	E	V	O	Ö	R	S
E	S	N	O	I	E	S	T	I	E	L	W	T	W
U	X	F	P	O	R	I	Y	C	T	D	E	U	E
K	D	H	D	Ä	T	L	O	H	N	E	U	N	R
L	R	J	E	Y	U	L	P	E	T	R	T	G	T
O	O	K	R	V	I	E	R	N	E	I	E	E	E

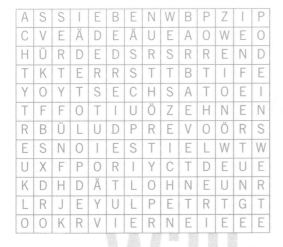 Willkommen

LANGUAGE FOCUS

The missing words in Exercise 5B are all verbs. Verbs follow certain patterns:

	kommen	*to come*
ich	komm**e**	*I come*
er/sie	komm**t**	*he/she comes*
Sie	komm**en**	*you come*

Irregular verbs **haben** (*to have*) and **sein** (*to be*) are exceptions:

	haben	**sein**
ich	habe	bin
er/sie	hat	ist
Sie	haben	sind

Try the additional activity on
www.accesslanguages.com

LEARNING TIP:

Sie has different meanings. In the question **Wie heißen Sie?** it means *What are you called?* **Sie** (always written with a capital letter) is the formal way of saying *you* in German. The convention is that if someone would like you to use anything but the formal **Sie**, they will let you know!

The other meaning you have met in this unit for **sie** is *she*.

7 Endungen

Complete the sentences below by changing the verb in brackets.

1 • Er ⟨_____⟩ Michael Patterson. (heißen)

2 • Ich ⟨_____⟩ aus Berlin. (kommen)

3 • Meine Mutter ⟨_____⟩ in Birmingham. (wohnen)

4 • Er ⟨_____⟩ in London. (wohnen)

5 • Wo ⟨_____⟩ Sie? (wohnen)

6 • Mein Baby ⟨_____⟩ Jasmin. (heißen)

7 • Sean Connery ⟨_____⟩ aus Schottland. (kommen)

8 • Der Mann ⟨_____⟩ ein Bier. (trinken)

8 Was wissen Sie über Ihre Kollegen?

A  Interview somebody in your group. Try and find out as much about them as you can. You already know these questions:

- Wo wohnen Sie?
- Wie heißen Sie?
- Wie ist Ihre Adresse?
- Wie ist Ihre Telefonnummer?

You could also ask:

- Was sind Ihre Hobbys?
- Wie viele Kinder haben Sie?

im Internet surfen

Musik

Inlineskating

Fotografieren

Schwimmen

Yoga

Tennis

Theater

Lesen

Willkommen

B Now report back to the class. Don't forget to change the verb.

1 • Er/sie **heißt** ( ).

2 • Seine/Ihre Adresse **ist** ( ).

3 • Er/Sie **wohnt** in ( ).

4 • Seine/Ihre Hobbys sind ( ) und ( ).

Beispiel:

Er heißt Paul. Er wohnt in Chester. Seine Hobbys sind Schwimmen und Fußball.

9 Fragewörter

  Question words

Decide whether to use **Wie?**, **Was?** or **Wo?**

1 • ( ) heißen Sie?

2 • ( ) ist Ihr Name?

3 • ( ) wohnt Ihre Mutter?

4 • ( ) wohnt die englische Königin?

5 • ( ) heißt die englische Königin?

6 • ( ) ist der Name von Tony Blairs Frau?

7 • ( ) heißt der amerikanische Präsident?

LANGUAGE FOCUS

Note the word order in questions that can only be answered 'yes' or 'no':

Wohnt er in Hamburg?   *Does he live in Hamburg?*
Haben Sie Kinder?   *Do you have any children?*

The verb comes first, followed by the subject.

10 Visitenkarten

Now work with your partner. Choose one of the business cards below without telling your partner which one. Ask questions that your partner can only answer with **ja** and **nein** but do not start with the name! Find out whose identity your partner has assumed.

Beispiel:

Wohnen Sie in Brügg?
Ist die Telefonnummer 331 0772?

Kosmetik-Institut

Marianne Keller
Rosengarten 4
9696 Ostermundigen
Tel. 032 331 07 72

SOLAR-STUDIO

Erika Gotzmann
Ahornweg 7
2555 Brügg
Tel. 032 373 42 66

Coiffure Sonja
S. Kodler
Kohlenstrasse 2
2876 Neuenstadt
tel. 032 331 07 72

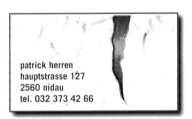

patrick herren
hauptstrasse 127
2560 nidau
tel. 032 373 42 66

Norbert Grolimund
Maurer
Kirchstrasse 43
8222 Develier
Tel. 032 331 07 72

11 Ein Reporter in Berlin

A Listen to some interviews with tourists in Berlin and complete the information in the table.

Vorname	Regina	Frank	–
Familienname	–	–	Schneider
Wohnt in	–	–	Zürich
Hobbys	–	–	–
Kinder	0 Kinder	–	–

B Compare your answers with your neighbour. Did you get all the information?

READY TO MOVE ON?

✓

Check that you can...

- ask and answer questions about where you live
- remember the verb endings for ich, Sie and er/sie
- say what your hobbies are
- remember the numbers 1–10
- say how many children you have.

12 Das Alphabet

A Listen to the alphabet and repeat it.

Note that the letters fit into a number of groups of similar sounds. This is because of the vowel sounds in the names of the letters:

- A, H, K
- B, C, D, E, G, P, T, W
- F, L, M, N, R, S, Z

- I, X
- J
- O

- Q, U
- V
- Y

B Work with a partner. Each of you makes a card with a different set of words like the ones below. Spell your words to your partner, and write your partner's words in a blank card. If you are not sure about a word, you can ask **Wie bitte?** or **Noch einmal, bitte?**

Partner A	Partner B	
lesen	Radio	
schwimmen	Vater	
Vorname	Adresse	
Telefon	trinken	
wohnen	Kinder	

C 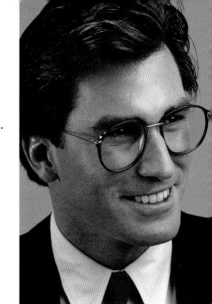 Now work with two other members of your group. Ask them to spell (**buchstabieren**) their names.

Beispiel:

– Wie heißen Sie?

– Frank Cook.

– Wie, bitte? Buchstabieren Sie, bitte.

– C-O-O-K.

GLOSSARY

There are many different ways of learning vocabulary. Find out what methods suit you best. You could, for example, write new vocabulary in your notebook and revise at home. Or you could copy new vocabulary onto 'Post-It' notes and distribute them throughout your house. Or what about recording them onto a cassette? Or copying new words onto little cards (English one side, German the other) and testing yourself? Whichever method you choose, repetition is the secret.

Nouns

Adresse (f)	address
Baby (n)	baby
Bier (n)	beer
Familienname (m)	surname
Frau (f)	woman, wife; also: Mrs
Hobbys (n, pl)	hobbies
Kind (n)	child
Musik (f)	music
Mutter (f)	mother
Name (m)	name
Ort (m)	place
Postleitzahl (f)	postcode
Staatsangehörigkeit (f)	nationality
Straße (f)	street
Telefonnummer (f)	telephone number
Tennis (n)	tennis
Theater (n)	theatre
Vorname (m)	first name

Willkommen

GLOSSARY

Adjectives

aktiv	active
amerikanisch	American
angenehm	pleasant
berühmt	famous
deutsch	German
englisch	English
jung	young

Verbs

heißen	to be called
(Internet) surfen	to surf (the Internet)
kommen	to come
schwimmen	to swim
sein	to be
spielen	to play
surfen	to surf (to windsurf)
trinken	to drink
wohnen	to live

Pronouns

ich	I
Sie	you (polite)
er	he
sie	she
mein(e)	my
Ihr(e)	your

Phrases

Angenehm.	Nice to meet you.
Auf Wiedersehen.	Goodbye.
Bitte.	Please.
Danke.	Thank you.
Guten Abend.	Hello (Good evening).
Guten Morgen.	Good morning.
Guten Tag.	Hello.
Noch einmal, bitte.	Please repeat.
Tschüs.	See you.

LOOKING FORWARD

UNIT 2
Was sind Sie von Beruf?

In Unit 2, we will be looking at jobs and professions. To prepare, look at the jobs listed below. Can you guess what they are? Is your job listed? Look up any jobs you can't guess in your dictionary, and your own if it's not listed.

Lehrer • Designer • Gärtner • Taxi-Fahrer • Angestellter • Sekretär • Rentner • Student • Bäcker • Kellner • Ingenieur

UNIT 2
Was sind Sie von Beruf?

> **By the end of this unit you will be able to:**
> - Introduce yourself and your job
> - Learn about finding a job
> - Use verb endings
> - Understand more signs and questions
> - Say the numbers up to 100
> - Understand the concept of genders in German

1 Wissen Sie noch?

In this section, you will revise what you learnt in Unit 1.

A  Write the correct number for each word.

vier		sieben		eins	
zwei		zehn		drei	
fünf		acht		neun	
sechs					

ACCESS GERMAN

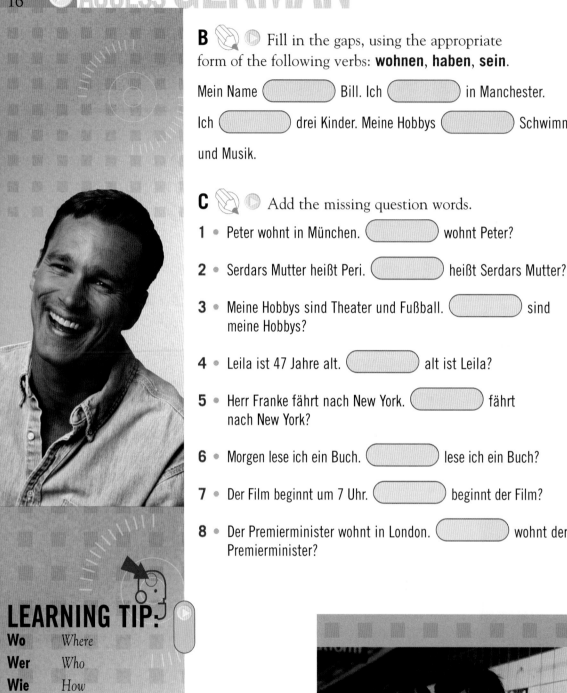

B Fill in the gaps, using the appropriate form of the following verbs: **wohnen**, **haben**, **sein**.

Mein Name ( ) Bill. Ich ( ) in Manchester.

Ich ( ) drei Kinder. Meine Hobbys ( ) Schwimmen

und Musik.

C Add the missing question words.

1 • Peter wohnt in München. ( ) wohnt Peter?

2 • Serdars Mutter heißt Peri. ( ) heißt Serdars Mutter?

3 • Meine Hobbys sind Theater und Fußball. ( ) sind meine Hobbys?

4 • Leila ist 47 Jahre alt. ( ) alt ist Leila?

5 • Herr Franke fährt nach New York. ( ) fährt nach New York?

6 • Morgen lese ich ein Buch. ( ) lese ich ein Buch?

7 • Der Film beginnt um 7 Uhr. ( ) beginnt der Film?

8 • Der Premierminister wohnt in London. ( ) wohnt der Premierminister?

LEARNING TIP:

Wo	*Where*
Wer	*Who*
Wie	*How*
Wann	*When*
Wohin	*Where to*

2 Was macht Peter?

Peter Schneider tells us about himself and his job. He gives quite a lot of information. Remember that at this stage we are listening out for specific information only. Do not try to understand every single word – it's the gist we are after.

A After listening once, decide which drawing is correct.

1

2

B Listen again and note down all the words from the list below that you can hear.

arbeiten Straße Kinder wohnen Haus lesen Hobby
Beruf drei vier Hamburg Name Film
schwimmen Popsänger Programmierer Buch Frau sie

Schlüsselwörter

von Beruf	*by profession*
Woche (f)	*week*
Jahr (n)	*year*
besuchen	*to visit*
aber	*but*
auch	*also, too*
interessant	*interesting*

C Listen one more time and note down which answer is correct. The key words on the left will help you understand and answer the questions.

1 • Wo wohnt Peter Schneider?
   a in Hamburg   **b** in Hannover   **c** in Berlin

2 • Was ist er von Beruf?
   a Lehrer   **b** Programmierer   **c** Hausmann

3 • Wie lange arbeitet er bei der Firma?
   a ein Jahr   **b** sieben Jahre   **c** vier Wochen

4 • Was sind seine Hobbys?
   a Computer   **b** Windsurfen   **c** Musik

5 • Wie viele Leute arbeiten bei der Firma?
   a neun   **b** 100   **c** zirca zehn

3 Was sind Sie von Beruf?

A Match these people with their professions.

1

2

3

4

5

6

a	Schauspielerin	**d**	Politikerin
b	Politiker	**e**	Schauspieler
c	Maler	**f**	Lehrerin

B Complete the table by filling in the professions from Exercise A.

♀	♂
Schauspielerin	

4 Lehrer oder Lehrerin?

Complete the sentences with the correct form of the word in brackets.

1 • Nadine ist _____ von Beruf. (teacher)

2 • Herr Schmidt arbeitet als _____ beim TV-Sender ARD. (actor)

3 • In der Galerie ist ein Bild von Tracey Emin. Sie ist eine _____, die schockiert. (painter)

4 • Mein Vater ist _____ an einer Schule in Essen. (teacher)

5 • Der Bundeskanzler ist _____. (politician)

6 • In Hollywood gibt es wenig Rollen für eine _____ über 40. (actress)

7 • Rembrandt war ein berühmter _____ im 17. Jahrhundert. (painter)

8 • Margaret Thatcher war die erste _____, die den Top-Job in England hatte. (politician)

LEARNING TIP:
The table above shows that most terms for professions have a female and a male version. The female version mostly has the ending **–in** added to the stem of the word.

Was sind Sie von Beruf? **UNIT** **2**

LANGUAGE FOCUS

die Limone

der Apfel

You will have noticed that some nouns have **die**, **der** or **das** in front of them. These show which gender the noun is. They all mean *the*:

die	*feminine*
der	*masculine*
das	*neuter*
die	*all plurals*

} the

The article (**der**, **die** or **das**) refers only to the *grammatical* gender and has nothing to do with the natural gender of the noun. For instance, in German, the word *girl* (**das Mädchen**) is neuter, not feminine.

There are definite (*the*) and indefinite (*a*) articles. (For more on the indefinite article, see page 55.) In the glossary at the end of the book, the gender of the noun is always indicated, and you will find rules and examples for noun genders in the grammar summary.

LEARNING TIP:

Always learn the gender of a new noun by learning the article along with the noun.

5 Mein Job

A  Have a look at the website below and decide which of the following you can expect to do:

- find a job
- find on-the-job training
- find a house

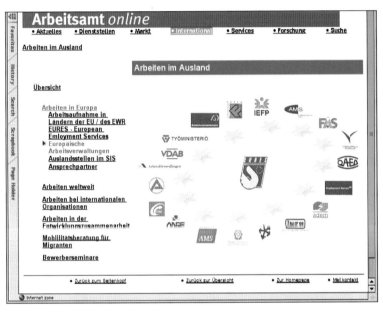

Arbeitsamt *online*

• Aktuelles • Dienststellen • Markt • International • Services • Forschung • Suche

Arbeiten im Ausland

Arbeiten im Ausland

Übersicht

Arbeiten in Europa
Arbeitsaufnahme in Ländern der EU / des EWR
EURES - European Emloyment Services
▶ Europäische Arbeitsverwaltungen
Auslandsstellen im SIS
Ansprechpartner

Arbeiten weltweit

Arbeiten bei internationalen Organisationen

Arbeiten in der Entwicklungszusammenarbeit

Mobilitätsberatung für Migranten

Bewerberseminare

• Zurück zum Seitenkopf   • Zurück zur Übersicht   • Zur Homepage   • Mail kontakt

Internet zone

B Look at the website again. Find the German words for the following words and expressions:

1 • all over the world
2 • in the countries of the EU
3 • search
4 • news
5 • working abroad
6 • research
7 • contact partner
8 • market

You'll find links to similar information sites and suggestions on how to use them to improve your German on our website.

UNIT **2**

21

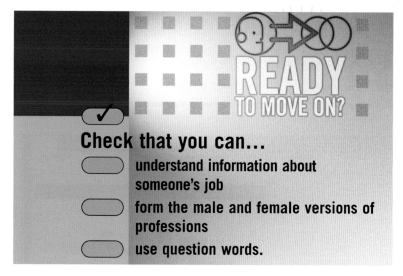

READY TO MOVE ON?

✓

Check that you can...

- understand information about someone's job
- form the male and female versions of professions
- use question words.

6 Ein Interview im Radio

A Listen to the radio interview and write down five words you can remember.

◯ ◯ ◯ ◯ ◯

B Listen to the interview again and decide if the sentences below are true (richtig) or false (falsch).

	Richtig	Falsch
1 • Herr Bayer arbeitet bei einer online banking Firma.	◯	◯
2 • Er arbeitet dort seit über zwei Jahren.	◯	◯
3 • Die Firma hat über 300 Mitarbeiter.	◯	◯
4 • Die Onlinebank hat eine virtuelle Assistentin.	◯	◯
5 • Online banking Firmen sind relativ neu.	◯	◯
6 • Online banking Firmen haben keine konventionellen Sekretärinnen.	◯	◯
7 • Die Advancebank arbeitet in ganz Deutschland.	◯	◯
8 • Die Advancebank arbeitet mit der Dresdner Bank zusammen.	◯	◯

7 Was machen Sie?

Talk to someone else in the class about your job, and ask what they do. Here are some expressions to help you.

Wo arbeiten Sie?	Ich arbeite bei ( ).
Was sind Sie von Beruf?	Ich bin ( ) von Beruf.
Als was arbeiten Sie?	Ich arbeite als ( ).
Wie lange arbeiten Sie schon bei ( ) / dieser Firma?	Ich arbeite seit ( ) Jahren/ seit 19( ) bei ( )/ der Firma ( ).
Was machen Sie in Ihrem Job?	Ich ( ).

8 Was macht Ihr Kollege?

Tell the rest of the class what you have found out about your partner. Remember to change the verb ending for *he/she* (**er/sie**).

( ) arbeitet bei ( ).

Er/Sie ist ( ) von Beruf.

Er/Sie arbeitet seit ( ) Jahren

bei ( ).

Er/Sie ( ).

LEARNING TIP:
Sie – du

Sie is the formal way of addressing someone, whereas **du** is more informal. Even though conventions are becoming more relaxed in Germany, it is always safer to use **Sie** rather than **du**.

Note that the verb form changes if you are using **du**, e.g. **Sie arbeiten** but **du arbeite*st***.

READY TO MOVE ON?

✓ Check that you can...

- ( ) talk about your job
- ( ) ask questions about someone else's job
- ( ) address someone informally and formally.

UNIT **2**

23

9 Die Zahlen 10–100

vierzehn

18

sechzehn

31

sechsundzwanzig

14

achtzehn

70

zwanzig   16

einunddreißig

20

siebzig

26

LANGUAGE FOCUS

After 11 and 12, numbers become very regular in German.

11	elf	19	neunzehn	40	vierzig
12	zwölf	20	zwanzig	50	fünfzig
13	dreizehn	21	einundzwanzig	60	sechzig
14	vierzehn	22	zweiundzwanzig	70	siebzig
15	fünfzehn	23	dreiundzwanzig	80	achtzig
16	sechzehn		↓	90	neunzig
17	siebzehn	29	neunundzwanzig	100	(ein)hundert
18	achtzehn	30	dreißig		

Note the omission of the 's' from sechs in sechzehn and sechzig, and the 'en' from sieben in siebzehn and siebzig.

Test yourself on the numbers on our website.

A 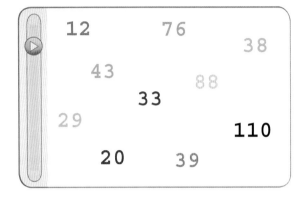 Read the numbers and match them with the correct figures.

dreiundvierzig	29
siebzehn	65
vierundvierzig	44
neunundzwanzig	**88**
dreißig	72
zweiundsiebzig	17
achtundachtzig	43
siebenundachtzig	87
fünfundsechzig	30

12   76   38
43   88
33
29   110
20   39

B Listen to the numbers and identify the ones you hear from the box above.

10 Telefonnummern

A Work with a partner. Ask each other questions based on the telephone numbers from the website. Try and read the numbers in tens or hundreds.

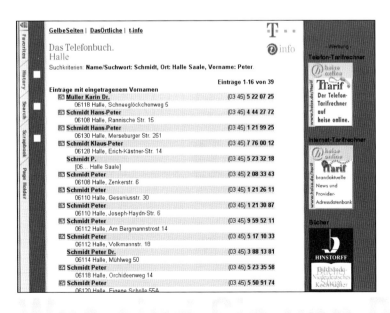

1 Wer hat die Telefonnummer (03 45) 121 26 11?

2 Welche Telefonnummer hat Klaus-Peter Schmidt?

3 Wie ist die Telefonnummer zu der Adresse Merseburger Straße 261?

Use the patterns in questions 1–3 to form some more questions.

B  Listen to the recording and decide which of the numbers below correspond to the ones you hear. Note that telephone numbers tend to be read in pairs.

1 • 2-29-57-87		**6** • 2-38-34-02	
2 • 2-85-98-68		**7** • 4-48-72-38	
3 • 3-43-47-29		**8** • 7-37-38-19	
4 • 8-81-26-15		**9** • 3-10-04-12	
5 • 2-24-17-82		**10** • 5-29-42-48	

GLOSSARY

Nouns

Bank (f)	bank	**Jahrhundert** (n)	century
Beruf (m)	profession	**Lehrer** (m)	teacher
Bild (n)	picture	**Maler** (m)	painter
Buch (n)	book	**Mitarbeiter** (m)	member of staff
Bundeskanzler (m)	chancellor (the German equivalent of the British Prime Minister)	**Politiker** (m)	politician
		Premierminister (m)	prime minister
		Programmierer (m)	programmer
		Rolle (f)	role
Film (m)	film	**Schauspieler** (m)	actor
Firma (f)	company	**Schule** (f)	school
Fußball (m)	football	**Sekretärin** (f)	secretary
Galerie (f)	gallery	**Sender** (m)	channel (TV or radio)
Haus (n)	house		
Hausmann (m)	house husband	**Vater** (m)	father
Jahr (n)	year	**Woche** (f)	week

GLOSSARY

Adjectives

interessant	interesting
neu	new
virtuell	virtual

Verbs

arbeiten	to work
beginnen	to start
besuchen	to visit
einkaufen	to shop
fahren	to go (by car or train)
fernsehen	to watch TV
haben	to have
hören	to listen
im Garten arbeiten	to garden
inlineskaten	to rollerblade
Klavier spielen	to play the piano
kochen	to cook
lesen	to read
machen	to make/to do
tanzen	to dance

LOOKING FORWARD

In Unit 3, we will be looking at hobbies and daily routines. To prepare, look at the words listed below. Can you guess what they mean? Is your hobby listed? Look up in your dictionary any hobbies you can't guess, and your own if it's not listed.

schwimmen • **tanzen** • **inlineskaten** • **lesen** • **fernsehen**
• **kochen** • **Computer spielen** • **im Garten arbeiten** • **einkaufen**
• **Musik hören** • **Klavier spielen**

UNIT 3
Meine Woche

UNIT

2

UNIT 3
Meine Woche

By the end of this unit you will be able to:

- Tell the time and ask what time it is
- Say the days of the week
- Express what you do during the week
- Understand and talk about a TV guide
- Use different verb forms
- Understand the concept of separable verbs
- Understand the concept of genders in German

LEARNING TIP:
The definite article (*the*) can either be **der**, **die** or **das**, depending on whether the noun is masculine, feminine or neuter. If you cannot remember the correct gender, look up the word in the glossary. If you cannot remember whether it is **der**, **die** or **das** when you are speaking, just guess – the word itself will still be understood!

1 Wissen Sie noch?

A Note down the correct article for each of these nouns.

1 • ( ) Beruf
2 • ( ) Tag
3 • ( ) Haus
4 • ( ) Firma
5 • ( ) Mitarbeiter

6 • ( ) Bank
7 • ( ) Assistentin
8 • ( ) Sekretärin
9 • ( ) Job
10 • ( ) Telefonnummer

B  Note down the correct figure for each number.

1 • vierhundert ⬭

2 • dreiundzwanzig ⬭

3 • sieben ⬭

4 • einhundertdreiundzwanzig ⬭

5 • achtundneunzig ⬭

6 • achthundertsiebzehn ⬭

7 • sechzehn ⬭

8 • dreihundertvierundachtzig ⬭

9 • eintausendvierhundertundzwölf ⬭

10 • neunundvierzig ⬭

LANGUAGE FOCUS

The days of the week in German are as follows:

Montag
Dienstag
Mittwoch
Donnerstag
Freitag
Samstag (*in some regions people say* Sonnabend)
Sonntag

They are all masculine (**der**).

Montag	1	8	15	22	29
Dienstag	2	9	16	23	30
Mittwoch	3	10	17	24	31
Donnerstag	4	11	18	25	
Freitag	5	12	19	26	
Samstag	6	13	20	27	
Sonntag	7	14	21	28	

Meine Woche UNIT 3

2 Hören Sie mal!

A Listen to the telephone conversation and decide which summary describes the conversation correctly.

1 • Karl rang Anna to discuss the project report she is preparing for Monday.

2 • Karl rang Anna to invite her to a concert at the Berlin Philharmonie the following Friday night.

B Listen to the conversation again, then choose the correct answer to the questions below.

1 • What is Anna doing when Karl phones?
   a She is on her way to a concert.
   b She is relaxing at home.
   c She is writing a project report for Monday.

2 • What did Karl phone Anna for?
   a He wants to go to the theatre.
   b He asks her out.
   c He offers to help her.

3 • What day of the week are they arranging to meet?
   a Saturday
   b Wednesday
   c Friday

4 • What time do they arrange to meet?
   a 8 p.m.
   b 7 p.m.
   c 7.30 p.m.

5 • Where do they decide to meet?
   a the bar
   b the Philharmonie
   c the bar at the Philharmonie

Practise inviting your German friends on www.accesslanguages.com

LANGUAGE FOCUS

When using the days of the week in a sentence to say when you are doing something, i.e. 'on Saturday', 'on Monday' etc., the correct German form is **am**:

- Am Dienstag gehe ich schwimmen. Am Mittwoch mache ich Aerobic.

Grammatically speaking, **am** is made up of **an + dem**

dem indicates a particular case of **der**, the dative case (you will learn more about the dative later on).

When inviting someone, e.g. to meet up, you can use the following expressions:

- Treffen wir uns ...
- Sagen wir um ...

C Listen to the telephone conversation once more and complete the gaps in the text below.

Heute ist Sonntag, aber Anna arbeitet zu Hause. Am ( ) muß sie einen Projektbericht abgeben. Karl hat zwei Tickets für ein ( ). Das Konzert ist am ( ). Anna und Karl treffen sich um ( ) in der Bar in der Philharmonie. Die Philharmonie ist ein berühmter Konzertsaal in Berlin.

UNIT **3**

3 Sie sind dran!

 ▶ Work with a partner for this activity. Choose one of the scenarios below and arrange to meet your partner.

Theater am Stadtpark
Hamlet
Mittwoch, 20 Uhr

Kino Odeon
Armageddon
Donnerstag, 19 Uhr

Faschingsparty bei Stefan
Samstag, 20 Uhr

Konzert
In der Stadtkirche
Händels Messias
Sonntag, 16 Uhr

4 So ein Durcheinander!

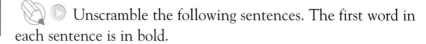 LANGUAGE FOCUS

In Unit 1, you learnt how to form a question with a question word. In this unit, we are focusing on some aspects of the *word order* of sentences. The main rule is that in German the verb always comes second. This does not necessarily mean that the verb is actually the second word – but it must be the second meaningful unit in the sentence. You often find the word or phrase that carries the main emphasis of the sentence in first place, e.g.:

* Ich   trinke   jeden Tag zwei Liter Wasser.
* Zwei Liter Wasser trinke   ich jeden Tag!

When the sentence contains words or expressions that tell you how, when or where something is being done, the expression of **time** usually comes first, **manner** second and **place** third. This is known as the 'time-manner-place' rule, e.g.:

* Ich fahre **jeden Tag**   **mit dem Auto**   **nach München.**
  time   manner   place

You'll find further activities on German word order on our website.

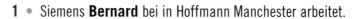 Unscramble the following sentences. The first word in each sentence is in bold.

1 • Siemens **Bernard** bei in Hoffmann Manchester arbeitet.

2 • in wohnt Mutter **Meine** Berlin.

3 • ich gehe ins Kino **Morgen**.

4 • spiele **Am** Badminton Montag ich.

5 • im **Meine** Lesen sind, Schwimmen, Garten Hobbys und arbeiten.

6 • ich **Jeden** gehe einkaufen Samstag.

7 • Lotto **Einmal** spielen im Monat wir.

8 • Wochen **Im** für fahren wir zwei nach August Frankreich.

9 • Auto Freundin hat **Meine** ein neues.

10 • **Jeden** Büro 'dressing down' Tag Freitag im ist.

5 Die Wochentage

Complete the crossword with the days of the week in German.

1 • Sunday (7)
2 • Tuesday (8)
3 • Saturday (7)
4 • Wednesday (8)
5 • Monday (6)
6 • Friday (7)
7 • Thursday (10)

Check that you can...

- remember the days of the week
- use them correctly in sentences
- understand word order in a German sentence and form sentences correctly.

ACCESS GERMAN

6 Meine Woche

Schlüsselwörter

viel zu tun haben	*to be busy*
vollberuflich	*full-time*
keine Zeit	*no time*
ein bisschen	*a little*

Many German magazines have online sites. You can start with the ones suggested on our website.

Read and listen to the following text, which was taken from a magazine interview about people's hobbies and their work/spare-time ratio.

Hallo. Mein Name ist Petra, und ich bin dreißig Jahre alt. Ich habe immer viel zu tun in der Woche und habe keine Zeit für Hobbys. Ich bin Ärztin von Beruf, und ich arbeite vollberuflich. Abends bin ich dann zu müde. Wenn ich ein bisschen Zeit habe, gehe ich gern schwimmen. Am Montag gibt es Schwimmen für Frauen um 20 Uhr. Am Sonntag gehe ich oft ins Kino.

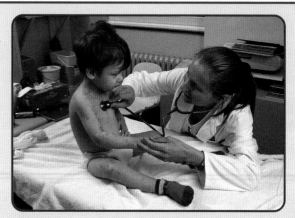

Hi. Ich heiße Jannis, und ich studiere Informatik an der Uni in Jena. Mein Hobby ist Computing und Informatik. Mittwochs und Freitags habe ich einen Nebenjob – ich arbeite an einer Datenbank für eine Kaufhaus-Kette in Thüringen.

Hallo. Mein Name ist Judith, und ich bin 62 Jahre alt. Seit September bin ich pensioniert und habe jetzt etwas mehr Zeit. Am Dienstag spiele ich mit meiner

Freundin Tennis. Erst haben wir eine Stunde Unterricht, und dann spielen wir ein Match. Freitags gehe ich immer einkaufen, und am Samstag kommen meine Enkel zu mir und bleiben über Nacht.

A [A C] ⊙ Now decide if the statements below are true or false.

	Richtig	**Falsch**
1 • Judith has the busiest social life.	⬭	⬭
2 • Petra goes swimming every Monday.	⬭	⬭
3 • Jannis goes shopping in a department store on Wednesdays and Fridays.	⬭	⬭
4 • Judith's grandchildren come to stay every Sunday.	⬭	⬭
5 • On Fridays, Judith goes shopping.	⬭	⬭

B [A C] ✎ ⊙ Read the texts again, then fill in the gaps in the summary below.

Petra arbeitet sehr viel. Sie ist Ärztin und hat keine Zeit für Hobbys. Manchmal geht sie am (＿＿＿＿＿＿＿) schwimmen. Jannis hat auch keine Zeit. Sein Hobby wird sein Beruf! Zweimal in der Woche, am (＿＿＿＿＿＿＿) und (＿＿＿＿＿＿＿), arbeitet er für eine Kaufhaus-Kette. Judith hat mehr Zeit. (＿＿＿＿＿＿＿) ist ihr Einkaufstag, und am (＿＿＿＿＿＿＿) spielt sie Tennis. Am (＿＿＿＿＿＿＿) hat sie immer ihre zwei Enkel zu Besuch.

7 Sie sind dran!

👥 🔊 ⊙ Prepare a little talk for your fellow students about what you do during the week. This is the perfect opportunity to invent the colourful and interesting life you have always wanted!

Am Montag …

Montag	8.00 Zahnarzt
Dienstag	🌀
Mittwoch	🌀
Donnerstag	19.00 Aerobics im Gemeindehaus
Freitag	🌀
Samstag	🌀
Sonntag	13.00 Mittagessen bei Klaus und Gabi

Meine Woche

LANGUAGE FOCUS

When describing an activity such as playing sport, the verb usually goes with another word, e.g. I play *football*, he plays *tennis*, etc. In German, the verb goes in second position and the other word (usually a noun) goes to the end of the clause. This gives the speaker the opportunity to vary the meaning of the sentence so that the phrase at the front carries more emphasis.

Ich	spiele	Fußball.
Jeden Sonntag	spiele ich	Fußball.
Ich	spiele	jeden Sonntag Fußball.

8 Fragen Sie Ihren Partner!

Find out what your partner does on different days of the week. There are two ways of asking for the information.

- You could ask what he or she does on a particular day of the week, e.g.: Was machen Sie am Mittwoch?

- You could ask when he or she does a particular activity: Wann spielen Sie Fußball? Wann trinken Sie Bier in der Kneipe?

Hobbys

fotografieren	*to take photos*
Computerspiele spielen	*to play computer games*
im Internet surfen	*to surf the Net*
Handarbeiten machen	*to do needlework*
ein Buch oder eine Zeitschrift lesen	*to read a book or a magazine*
fernsehen	*to watch TV*
ins Kino gehen	*to go to the cinema*
tanzen	*to dance*

Some verbs are separable and come in two parts, e.g. **fernsehen = sehen + fern** (literally: *to see far*). When these are used in a sentence, the main part of the verb goes in second position, and the other part is sent to the end. Very often this part is a preposition which, added to a verb, changes the meaning, e.g.:

kaufen   *to buy*
einkaufen   *to shop*
abkaufen   *to buy off (someone)*

If there is nothing to follow in the sentence, the main part of the verb comes after the subject and the other part is split from it:

einkaufen: ich kaufe ein (*I shop*)
radfahren: wir fahren Rad (*we cycle*)
fernsehen: er sieht fern (*he watches TV*)

When there is something to follow, the separable part goes to the end of the sentence:

Er sieht jeden Abend fern.
He watches TV every evening.

Don't worry – with time you will start to recognise these verbs and know how to use them.

Note that some verbs – including separable verbs – undergo a vowel change in the third person singular, e.g:

fahren   er fährt
anfangen   er fängt an
fernsehen   er sieht fern

9 Gehen wir ins Theater?

Put the verbs from the box in the correct position in the sentence.
Be careful – in some sentences there are two gaps in the text but only one verb.

1 • Am Freitag ⬭⬭⬭⬭ ich immer ⬭⬭⬭ .

2 • Mein Schwiegervater ⬭⬭⬭⬭⬭ jeden Tag

    drei Stunden im Garten.

3 • ⬭⬭⬭⬭ du mit ins Kino?

4 • Wann ⬭⬭⬭ das Konzert ⬭⬭ ?

5 • Wann ⬭⬭⬭ der Zug nach Hamburg?

6 • Wo ⬭⬭ die Nationalgalerie?

7 • Mein Sohn ⬭⬭⬭ immer ⬭⬭⬭ .

8 • Die meisten Kinder ⬭⬭⬭⬭ zu viel Computerspiele.

ausgehen   anfangen

fernsehen

              arbeiten

kommen

       sein

fahren   spielen

UNIT **3**

READY TO MOVE ON?

✓

Check that you can...

- talk about and ask someone about what they do on individual days
- remember the days of the week
- use separable verbs correctly.

10 Noch mehr Hobbys

A 🎲 ✏️ ▶️ Look at the website below. What would you expect to find on this site? Note down three key words in German:

- _____
- _____
- _____

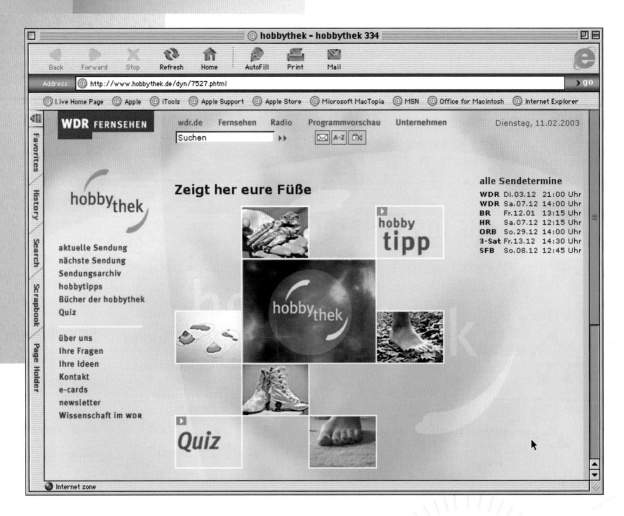

B [A C] 🖐 (🎧) ▷ Read the following introduction and answer the questions below.

Hobbythek ist eine Fernsehserie im WDR (der Westdeutsche Rundfunk). Die Sendung gibt Tipps für verschiedene Hobbys. Man kann Tipps zu vielen Themen finden, zum Beispiel zu diesen Themen:

- Geheimnisse der italienischen Küche
- Besser schlafen
- Gesund wohnen
- Ayurveda

Jedes Thema hat eine Sendung. Ein oder zwei Reporter geben Informationen und Tipps zum Thema. In der Sendung 'Geheimnisse der italienischen Küche' erfährt der Zuschauer mehr über die regionale Küche in Italien. Man sieht die Landschaft und die Menschen. Im Studio gibt es dann ein paar Rezepte mit allen Zutaten, natürlich den bekannten italienischen Klassischen Zutaten wie Auberginen, Tomaten, Zucchini, Pasta, Parmesan und viel mehr. Die Sendung kommt zweimal im Monat, und viele Leute schalten jedes Mal ein.

1 • What is Hobbythek?
2 • Where can it be seen?
3 • What do the presenters do?
4 • Can you remember three topics?
5 • What would you see in the programme about Italian cuisine?

C [A C] ▷ Look at the website in Exercise A again and say which option you would choose in order to …

1 • search
2 • find out the schedule for programmes
3 • get to the page on frequently asked questions (FAQs)
4 • look up books
5 • find out about the programme-makers
6 • get a complete listing

D 🖐 ▷ Write an e-mail to the Hobbythek people asking for recipe details from the programme on Italian cuisine. Ask what ingredients you need for ratatouille.

Meine Woche UNIT 3

Don't forget to browse through our list of German hobby websites on www.accesslanguages.com

11 Wann kommt die Hobbythek?

A Have a look at the programme listing below.

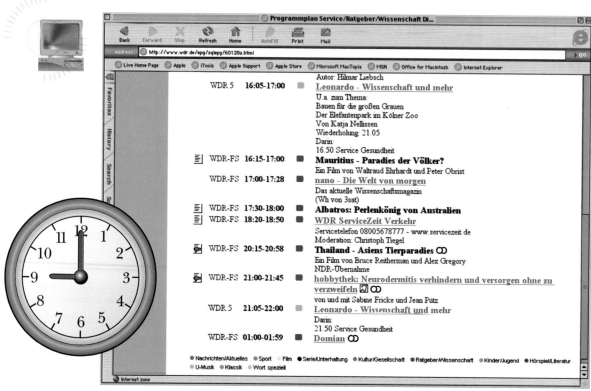

```
                                    Autor: Hilmar Liebsch
        WDR 5    16:05-17:00        Leonardo - Wissenschaft und mehr
                                    U.a. zum Thema:
                                    Bauen für die großen Grauen
                                    Der Elefantenpark im Kölner Zoo
                                    Von Katja Nellissen
                                    Wiederholung: 21.05
                                    Dann:
                                    16.50 Service Gesundheit

        WDR-FS   16:15-17:00        Mauritius - Paradies der Völker?
                                    Ein Film von Waltraud Ehrhardt und Peter Obrist
        WDR-FS   17:00-17:28        nano - Die Welt von morgen
                                    Das aktuelle Wissenschaftsmagazin
                                    (Wh von 3sat)

        WDR-FS   17:30-18:00        Albatros: Perlenkönig von Australien
        WDR-FS   18:20-18:50        WDR ServiceZeit Verkehr
                                    Servicetelefon 08005678777 · www.servicezeit.de
                                    Moderation: Christoph Tiegel

        WDR-FS   20:15-20:58        Thailand - Asiens Tierparadies
                                    Ein Film von Bruce Reitherman und Alex Gregory
                                    NDR-Übernahme

        WDR-FS   21:00-21:45        hobbythek: Neurodermitis verhindern und versorgen ohne zu
                                    verzweifeln
                                    von und mit Sabine Fricke und Jean Pütz

        WDR 5    21:05-22:00        Leonardo - Wissenschaft und mehr
                                    Dann:
                                    21.50 Service Gesundheit

        WDR-FS   01:00-01:59        Domian
```

● Nachrichten/Aktuelles ● Sport ● Film ● Serie/Unterhaltung ● Kultur/Gesellschaft ● Ratgeber/Wissenschaft ● Kinder/Jugend ● Hörspiel/Literatur
● U-Musik ● Klassik ● Wort speziell

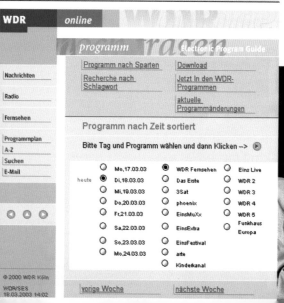

Die Hobbythek kommt am Dienstag um 21 Uhr.

Was kommt davor? Um 20 Uhr 15 kommt ein Dokumentarfilm über Thailand.

Was kommt danach? Um 21 Uhr 05 kommt ...

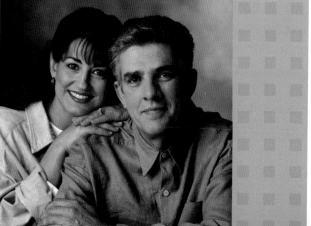

In Germany and German-speaking countries, the 24-hour clock is used frequently. From a language point of view it is very easy to use:

17.00 Uhr   siebzehn Uhr
17.45 Uhr   siebzehn Uhr fünfundvierzig

Using the 12-hour clock is very similar to English:

7.45   viertel vor acht
8.15   viertel nach acht
8.20   zwanzig nach acht
7.50   zehn vor acht

The only difference is that 'half' the hour indicates half *before* the hour rather than half past.

9.30   halb zehn
3.30   halb vier

Remember:
Germans do not use an equivalent for a.m. or p.m. – the context will make clear what time of day is referred to.

B   Wann kommt ...?

Choose a programme from the WDR website on the previous page, and ask your partner when it starts.

| **Wann kommt ...?** | ... **kommt um** ... **(Uhr).** |

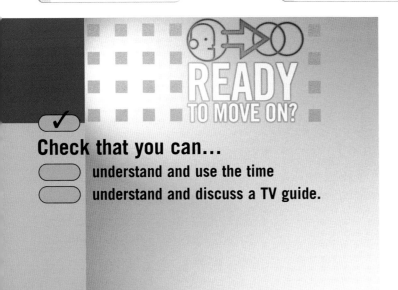

READY
TO MOVE ON?

✓

Check that you can...
understand and use the time
understand and discuss a TV guide.

12 Üben Sie!

Write the times.

1 `18:27`

2  `12:10`

3 `22:40`

4 `08:30`

5 `14:45`

6 `17:20`

7 `20:25`

8 `15:50`

9 `23:13`

10 `10:30`

GLOSSARY

Nouns

Assistentin (f)	female assistant
Datenbank (f)	database
Dienstag (m)	Tuesday
Donnerstag (m)	Thursday
Fasching (m)	carnival
Freitag (m)	Friday
Job (m)	job
Kaufhaus-Kette (f)	department-store chain
Kino (n)	cinema
Konzert (n)	concert
Konzertsaal (m)	concert hall
Mittwoch (m)	Wednesday
Montag (m)	Monday
Projektbericht (m)	project report
Samstag (m)	Saturday
Sonnabend (m)	Saturday
Sonntag (m)	Sunday
Stadtkirche (f)	church (lit. city church)
Stadtpark (m)	inner-city park
Tag (m)	day
Unterricht (m)	tuition

Adjectives

müde	tired
vollberuflich	full-time

Verbs

abgeben	to hand in
müssen	must (modal verb)
(sich) treffen	to meet (reflexive)
studieren	to study
wissen	to know

GLOSSARY

Phrases

ein bisschen	a little
heute	today
jeden Tag	every day
keine Zeit	no time
So ein Durcheinander!	What confusion!
viel zu tun haben	to be busy
Wissen Sie noch?	Do you remember?
zu Hause	at home

Conjunctions

aber	but

LOOKING FORWARD

In Unit 4, we will be looking at shopping and getting around a town. To prepare, look at the website below and find out what you can buy through this site. List at least four items in English.

UNIT 4
Wo ist das Hotel?

Meine Woche

3

UNIT 4
Wo ist das Hotel?

By the end of this unit you will be able to:

- Understand simple information about hotels
- Understand directions
- Ask for directions
- Familiarise yourself with the euro currency
- Ask for and understand prices
- Use cardinal numbers (1st, 2nd, 3rd)
- Use indefinite articles (*a*)
- Give instructions

We suggest that you come back to this checklist as you progress through the unit. You can then judge how you are getting on.

1 Wissen Sie noch?

A 🎲 ▶ Look at the verbs below and decide which verb goes with which sentence. Remember that some verbs are separable and some are not.

1 • Der Laden ist aber teuer! Hier ( ) ich nicht ( ).

2 • Herr Müller ( ) einen Secondhand-Computer.

3 • Sie wollen nach Hannover? Der Zug ( ) von Bahnsteig 3 ( ).

4 • Für Braunschweig ( ) Sie in Hannover ( ).

5 • Kinder, ( ) gut ( )!

6 • Der Zug aus London ( ) um 19.55 ( ).

7 • Schnell, Martin, der Zug ( )
in einer Minute ( ).

8 • Wann ( )
Stavros und Aischa?

umsteigen	**verkaufen**
kommen	**zuhören**
einkaufen	**abfahren**
abfahren	**ankommen**

B 🎲 ▶ Match the times with the numbers.

18.25 •	acht Uhr zwanzig
20.05 •	fünfzehn Uhr fünf
12.00 •	zwanzig Uhr fünf
6.30 •	vierzehn Uhr fünfundvierzig
19.30 •	neunzehn Uhr dreißig
9.15 •	achtzehn Uhr fünfundzwanzig
22.17 •	neun Uhr fünfzehn
14.45 •	zweiundzwanzig Uhr siebzehn
8.20 •	zwölf Uhr
15.05 •	sechs Uhr dreißig

LEARNING TIP:
Note that the prefix **ver-** does not split from the verb.

LEARNING TIP:
Braunschweig is a town in northern Germany.

Wo ist das Hotel? **UNIT 4**

2 Hören Sie mal!

A Listen to the dialogue and note down all the words you hear from the box.

> erkannt verheiratet verlobt geschieden
> kaufen beruflich Hobbys Marketing
> zum Beispiel Wohnung Hotel Firma Zimmer
> Präsentation Vertrag Kunde kennen Mädchen
> Appartements lesen einkaufen arbeiten
> trinken schlafen Wohnzimmer

B Listen to the dialogue again and answer the multiple-choice questions.

1 • What do you find out about Gabi's marital status?
  a She is married.
  b She is divorced.
  c She is engaged.

2 • How many children does Christian have?
  a three
  b two
  c one

3 • What does Gabi do for a living?
  a She works for a national marketing company.
  b She owns a marketing company.
  c She works in Frankfurt.

4 • What is she doing next week?
  a She is going to Magdeburg.
  b She is going to England.
  c She is going to Berlin.

5 • What is she doing there?
  a She is doing a presentation for a new customer.
  b She is attending a conference in Berlin.
  c She is going on holiday.

3 Wir suchen ein Hotel!

A Look at the adjectives below and decide which three are unlikely to describe a hotel room.

zentral	langsam	teuer
bequem	spät	sauer
laut	hell	modern
klein		

B Use the remaining seven adjectives from Exercise A to complete the sentences below.

1 • Das Hotel ist in der Friedrichstrasse – sehr (_____).

2 • Ein Doppelzimmer kostet €130 pro Nacht. Für Berlin ist das nicht sehr (_____).

3 • Das Hotel ist zwei Jahre alt, und die Architektur ist (_____).

4 • Das Bett ist (_____).

5 • Das Hotel hat viel Glas. Das macht die Zimmer (_____).

6 • Das Hotel ist direkt in der Friedrichstrasse. Dort fahren viele Autos, und das ist manchmal (_____).

7 • Das Restaurant hat nur sechs Tische. Das ist sehr (_____).

C Now look at the home page of a hotel in Munich (München) on page 48. Which of the following items are mentioned?

- 115 rooms
  - comfortable rooms
- gourmet restaurant
  - located centrally
  - 15 minutes from the station on foot
- squash court
  - well-equipped fitness studio
  - beauty salon
  - swimming pool

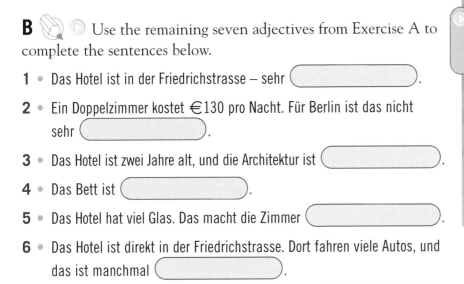

Schlüsselwörter	
nicht nur …, sondern auch	*not only … , but*
genießen	*to enjoy*
auch	*also*

You'll find additional practice in asking about accommodation on our website.

Wo ist das Hotel? UNIT 4

ACCESS GERMAN

Willkommen im Asam Hotel im Zentrum Münchens. Hier finden Sie alles was Sie für einen Aufenthalt in München brauchen. Wir haben bequeme und moderne Zimmer und ein Gourmet-Restaurant. In unserem 3-Sterne-Restaurant können Sie nicht nur frühstücken, sondern auch ein romantisches Abendessen bei Kerzenlicht in der Münchner Innenstadt genießen.

Das Hotel ist sehr zentral und einfach zu finden. Vom Bahnhof bis zum Hotel dauert es nur fünfzehn Minuten zu Fuß.

Für Fitness-Fans hat unser Hotel auch alles, was Sie brauchen: Sie können das Fitness-Center besuchen. Auch das ist modern ausgestattet mit einem Swimming Pool und einer Sauna.

Wir freuen uns auf Ihren Besuch!

Vor- und nach einem aufregenden Tag, einem unvergeßlichen Abend - sich zu Hause fühlen.

das asam - im Herzen Münchens!

Erleben sie Ihren Aufenthalt in einer Atmosphäre der Ruhe und Gelassenheit. Sympatisch und behaglich!

Ideal für Ihren München Business-Aufenthalt, Opernbesuch, Messe/Konzert/Theater/Fußball, zum Shopping und natürlich zum Oktoberfest.

4 Wo ist das Hotel?

A 🎲 👂 Look at the map of Berlin and locate 'Unter den Linden'. Find three famous landmark sights.

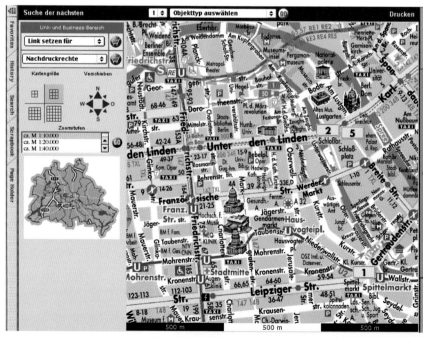

To find your way around in Germany, you will need to be able to ask for and understand directions.

Position

links	*left*
rechts	*right*
auf der linken Seite	*on the left-hand side*
auf der rechten Seite	*on the right-hand side*

Direction

nach links	*to the left*
nach rechts	*to the right*
geradeaus	*straight on*

How to use Sie

The verb comes first in the sentence, then **Sie**, followed by the actual directions:

Gehen Sie nach rechts.
Nehmen Sie die erste Straße links.
Gehen Sie nach links.
Fahren Sie nach München.

How to use du

When addressing someone as **du**, such as a child or someone with whom you are on familiar terms, the instruction verb is formed by using the **du** verb form.

Drop the **du** and the **-st**:

du gehst ⟶ geh
du nimmst ⟶ nimm

But be careful – there are no umlauts (**ü, ä, ö**) in the imperative:

du fährst ⟶ fahr

Geh nach rechts.
Nimm die erste Straße links.
Geh nach links.
Fahr nach München.

Sometimes the verb is prefaced with **dann** (*then*):

Gehen Sie nach rechts.
Dann nehmen Sie die dritte Straße rechts.

Cardinal numbers

die **erste** Straße links	*first*
die **zweite** Straße rechts	*second*
die **dritte** Straße links	*third*

From the fourth cardinal number, the pattern becomes very regular:

vier**te**
fünf**te**
sechs**te**

Wo ist das Hotel? UNIT 4

B 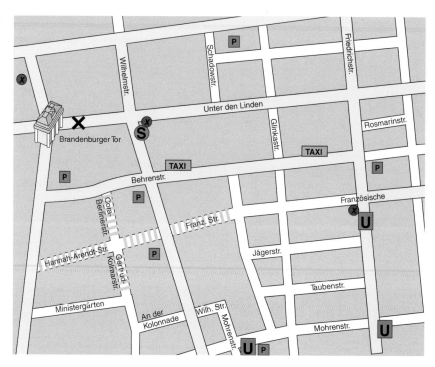 Listen to the conversation, look at the map below and follow the directions. What street is the hotel in?

(map showing Brandenburger Tor, Unter den Linden, Behrenstr., Franz. Str., Wilhelmstr., Schadowstr., Friedrichstr., Rosmarinstr., Glinkastr., Franzöische, Jägerstr., Taubenstr., Mohrenstr., Hannah-Arendt-Str., Ministergärten, An der Kolonnade, Wilh. Str., Gertrud-Kolmarstr., Cora-Berlinerstr.)

C Listen to the conversation again, follow the directions on the map, then recount them to your partner.

5 Wie komme ich zum …?

A What is missing in these directions?

1 • Gehen Sie ( ) rechts.

2 • ( ) Sie nach links.

3 • Nehmen Sie die erste ( ) links.

4 • Geh sofort ( ) links.

5 • ( ) Sie die dritte Straße rechts.

6 • Gehen Sie ( )

7 • (_____) die vierte Straße links.

8 • Das Hotel ist auf der linken (_____).

B 🎲 🔊 ▶ Look at the signs on the right and formulate directions.

C 🎲 🔊 👥 ▶ Try out your map-reading skills! Look at the map and locate a destination. Give your partner directions to follow and ask where he or she ends up.

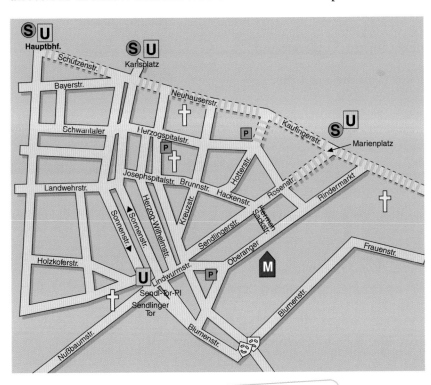

Surf some German map sites. You'll find suggestions on our website.

6 Wo ist … ?

🔊 👥 You are a tourist in Berlin and you are at the Berliner Dom. Ask your partner questions, then swap roles. Check the map on page 48 for directions.

Tourist:
Entschuldigen Sie, wo ist
… die Nationalgalerie?
… die Komische Oper?
… das Berliner Ensemble?

Berliner:
Gehen Sie nach …
Nehmen Sie die erste/zweite/
dritte Straße rechts/links.
Gehen Sie …

UNIT **4**

51

7 Ein Tourist in Berlin

Listen to the dialogue and decide which of the statements are true (richtig) and which are false (falsch).

	Richtig	Falsch
1 • The tourist is asking the way to Friedrichstraße.	⬭	⬭
2 • The man suggests taking the Underground.	⬭	⬭
3 • The Underground stop is near Brandenburger Tor.	⬭	⬭
4 • He tells the tourist to go on the Underground for four stops.	⬭	⬭
5 • He gives the tourist a ticket for the Underground.	⬭	⬭
6 • The tourist can get a ticket from the machine.	⬭	⬭

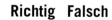

Berlin has many official and unofficial websites. Some of the best are listed on our website.

LANGUAGE FOCUS

In Unit 3, you learnt about separable verbs.

The imperative (used for giving someone instructions) for separable verbs is based on familiar rules. The prefix is split up from the main part of the verb and sent to the end.

aufstehen (*to get up*) ⟶ Stehen Sie auf!
zuhören (*to listen closely*) ⟶ Hören Sie zu!

Adding **bitte** to the phrase changes the imperative into a more polite request.

Stehen Sie bitte auf.
Hören Sie bitte zu.

8 Wissen Sie, wo Sie sind?

You are going to hear four sets of directions. Look at the map on the next page and decide where they lead you to.

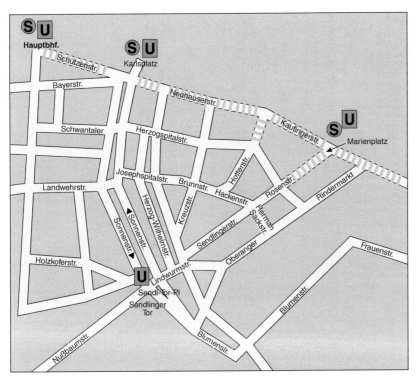

1 •
2 •
3 •
4 •

READY
TO MOVE ON?

✓

Check that you can...

- ask for directions
- understand directions
- give directions
- understand the changes to the verb for giving instructions (imperative).

UNIT **4**

9 Ist hier eine Apotheke?

A 🔲 ▶ When travelling, there are usually a number of facilities a tourist needs. Try and match up the pictures with the words below.

1

2

3

4

5

6

7

8

a • eine Arztpraxis   d • ein Restaurant   g • eine Bank

b • ein Fahrscheinautomat   e • ein Parkplatz   h • ein Supermarkt

c • ein Briefkasten   f • eine Apotheke

B  Look at the list of nouns and sort them into a table like the one below. If you do not know the gender of the noun, look it up in the glossary or a dictionary.

masculine	feminine	neuter
der Stadtpark	die Marienkirche	das Parkhaus

Straße	Platz	Museum
Kaufhaus	Pizzeria	Brücke
Denkmal	Bahnhof	Garten
Zoo	U-Bahn-Station	Straßenbahn-Haltestelle
Universität	Opernhaus	Bibliothek
Galerie	Touristeninformation	Hotel

LANGUAGE FOCUS

Indefinite articles

So far, you have been using definite articles with nouns, i.e. **der**, **die** and **das**. These all equate to the English *the*. There are, however, also indefinite articles which mean *a*. The use of definite and indefinite articles in English and German is very similar, which should make them easier to use.

Not surprisingly, since there are three genders in German, there are also three different indefinite articles:

masculine: ein
feminine: eine
neuter: ein

As in English, there is no indefinite article in the plural.

Gender	definite article (*the*)	indefinite article (*a*)
Masculine	der	ein
Feminine	die	eine
Neuter	das	ein
Plural	die	–

Wo ist das Hotel? UNIT 4

C For this part of the activity, work with a partner. Pick a building or facility from the list on the previous page and ask your partner if there is one nearby.

Beispiel:

(**A**) Ist hier … in der Nähe?

(**B**) Ja, gehen Sie geradeaus und dann links, ungefähr 200 Meter.

10 Sie sind der Tourist!

You are the tourist. Ask for directions to get to the right place.

1 • Sie sind in Dresden und brauchen ein Zimmer.

2 • Sie sind im Hotel und haben Hunger.

3 • Sie haben Postkarten und brauchen Briefmarken.

4 • Sie wollen parken und brauchen ein Ticket.

5 • Sie sind im Hotel, und das Zimmer ist in der vierten Etage.

6 • Sie fahren mit dem Zug von Dresden nach Berlin.

7 • Sie haben Hunger und wollen ein Sandwich kaufen.

8 • Sie haben Migräne und brauchen Tabletten.

LANGUAGE FOCUS

You are sorry or would like to apologise.

Entschuldigen Sie, …   *Excuse me …*
Entschuldigung, …   *Excuse me …*

Es tut mir sehr/schrecklich/wahnsinnig leid.   *I am very/awfully/dreadfully sorry.*

11 Ein Fax aus Deutschland

Schlüsselwörter

dazwischen kommen	*to go wrong, to crop up*
sich freuen	*to look forward, to be pleased*
sich kennenlernen	*to meet, to get to know*
vorbei	*past*
die Panne	*the breakdown*

Brian Thompson is going to Berlin to visit the German head office. He was going to be picked up from the station by a German colleague, but something has cropped up and he received the following fax.

Read the fax below and then decide if the statements on the next page are true (**richtig**) or false (**falsch**).

Globales Design
Wilhelmstraße 112
10117 Berlin

Tel.: (030) 229 42 72
www.globalesdesign.de

Berlin, 28. April

Lieber Herr Thompson,

Leider ist etwas dazwischen gekommen, und ich kann Sie nun doch nicht vom Bahnhof abholen. Ich hatte eine Panne, und mein Auto ist in der Werkstatt.

Der Termin ist in unserem Büro in der Wilhelmstraße. Sie können es ganz leicht finden. Nehmen Sie den Flug-Bus vom Flughafen Tegel, und fahren Sie bis zum Ernst-Reuter-Platz. Das dauert ungefähr zwanzig Minuten. Dort steigen Sie in die U-Bahn Richtung Pankow (Vineta-Straße) und fahren bis zur Mohrenstraße. Wenn Sie aus der U-Bahn kommen, gehen Sie nach rechts am Supermarkt vorbei. Das ist die Wilhelmstraße. Gehen Sie dann ungefähr fünfhundert Meter Richtung Brandenburger Tor. Unser Büro ist auf der rechten Seite, Hausnummer 112, im dritten Stock.

Es tut mir sehr leid, daß ich Sie nicht abholen kann, aber ich freue mich darauf, Sie kennenzulernen.

Bis zum 7. Mai verbleibe ich mit freundlichen Grüßen,

Ihre Sabine Schneider

Wo ist das Hotel?

Richtig Falsch

1 • Brian is advised that he can catch a bus from the airport in Tegel.

2 • The journey from Tegel to Ernst-Reuter-Platz will take about forty minutes.

3 • From Ernst-Reuter-Platz, he needs to catch a tram.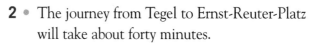

4 • At Mohrenstraße he will need to go past the Chinese restaurant.

5 • He will then have to turn left.

6 • He has to walk towards the Brandenburg Gate.

7 • After about 500 metres, the office is on the right.

8 • The office is on the second floor.

12 Sie sind dran!

Write a fax to a German colleague who is due to visit. Give her directions from the station to the town hall.

13 Kaufen Sie eine Fahrkarte!

Was kostet eine U-Bahn-Fahrkarte?

A Look at the different tariffs for Underground tickets in Berlin on the next page, then match the prices (1–8) with the different types of ticket (a–h).

U-Bhf Frankfurter Tor

Die Tarife im Überblick

Tarif Berlin	Teil- bzw. Tarifbereich	Preise in EURO
Kurzstrecke		1,20
Kurzstrecke, ermäßigt		1,00
Einzelfahrausweise	Berlin AB Berlin BC Berlin ABC	2,10 2,10 2,40
Einzelfahrausweise, ermäßigt	Berlin AB Berlin BC Berlin ABC	1,40 1,50 1,80
Anschlussfahrausweise	Berlin A	1,30
Tageskarte	Berlin AB Berlin BC Berlin ABC	6,10 6,10 6,30
Tageskarte, ermäßigt	Berlin AB Berlin BC Berlin ABC	4,10 4,10 4,50
Kleingruppenkarte (ab 1.8.2002)	Berlin AB Berlin BC Berlin ABC	15,00 15,00 16,00
Gruppentageskarten für Schüler ab 10 Schüler (pro Person)	Berlin AB Berlin ABC	2,00 3,00

1 sechs Euro zehn
2 ein Euro achtzig
3 vier Euro zehn
4 zwei Euro vierzig
5 ein Euro zwanzig
6 zwei Euro
7 ein Euro fünfzig
8 ein Euro

a eine Kurzstrecke
b eine Gruppentageskarte
c eine Kurzstrecke ermäßigt
d eine Tageskarte (AB)
e eine Tageskarte ermäßigt
f ein Einzelfahrausweis ermäßigt (ABC)
g ein Einzelfahrausweis (ABC)
h ein Einzelfahrausweis ermäßigt (BC)

B  Work with a partner. Look at the tariffs again and ask how much a particular ticket is.

(A) Was kostet eine Tageskarte?

(B) Eine Tageskarte kostet ....

LEARNING TIP:

To find out a price you can ask:

Was kostet … ?

or

Wieviel kostet … ?

The introduction of the euro has meant that shopping is much easier in most countries on the European mainland. Watch out for the German pronunciation of the euro: 'OY-roh'!

Note that there is no plural: 1 Euro, 30 Euro

NEU!
Ab 1. Juli auch am Automaten.

Flexibel, flexibel:
die gleitenden Monatskarten – jederzeit kaufen, einen Monat fahren!

GLOSSARY

Nouns

Apotheke (f)	chemist's, pharmacy
Arztpraxis (f)	doctor's surgery
Auto (n)	car
Bibliothek (f)	library
Briefkasten (m)	post box
Briefmarke (f)	postage stamp
Brücke (f)	bridge
Denkmal (n)	monument
Etage (f)	floor (as in first, second, etc.)
Fahrscheinautomat (m)	ticket machine
Flug (m)	flight
Flughafen (m)	airport
Gallerie (f)	gallery
Garten (m)	garden
Haltestelle (f)	station, stop
Hausnummer (f)	house number
Hotel (n)	hotel
Kaufhaus (n)	department store
Migräne (f)	migraine
Museum (n)	museum
Opernhaus (n)	opera house
Panne (f)	something wrong with the car, beakdown
Parkuhr (f)	parking meter
Parkplatz (m)	parking space
Pizzeria (f)	pizza restaurant
Platz (m)	square
Postkarte (f)	postcard
Richtung (f)	direction
Seite (f)	side, page
Station (f)	station, stop
Stock (m)	(here) floor (first, second, etc.)
Touristen-information (f)	tourist information
Universität (f)	university
Werkstatt (f)	garage
Zimmer (n)	room
Zoo (m)	zoo
Zug (m)	train

Adjectives

bequem	comfortable
klein	small, little
laut	noisy
zentral	central

Verbs

abfahren	to depart
abholen	to fetch (someone or something)
ankommen	to arrive
besuchen	to visit
brauchen	to need
einkaufen	to shop
(sich) freuen (auf)	to look forward to (reflexive verb)
genießen	to enjoy
kennenlernen	to meet

GLOSSARY

nehmen	to take
umsteigen	to change (trains, planes, etc.)
verkaufen	to sell
zuhören	to listen (to)

Adverbs
ungefähr	approximately

Phrases
Hunger haben	to be hungry
leider	unfortunately

LOOKING FORWARD

In Unit 5, we will be looking at some more shopping as well as food and drink. To prepare, look at the menu below and find four dishes that you recognise.

Café Orange
Speisekarte

Vorspeisen:	
Käseteller	7,50€
Frische Champignons, überbacken	6,00€
Nudelgerichte:	
Tagliatelle Gorgonzolasauce	7,00€
Spaghetti Carbonera	5,50€
Pizza:	
Pizza Champignon	5,50€
Pizza Calzone	7,50€
Dessert – Kuchen – Eis:	
Gemischtes Eis	3,50€
Pfirsich Melba	4,00€

UNIT 5
Im Restaurant

UNIT 4

UNIT 5
Im Restaurant

By the end of this unit you will be able to:

- Go shopping in a supermarket
- Talk about food and drink
- Ask for and understand prices
- Form the plural of nouns
- Understand the accusative case
- Order a meal

We suggest that you come back to this checklist as you progress through the unit. You can then judge how you are getting on.

1 Wissen Sie noch?

A Trennbare Verben. Read the sentences on the next page and extract the verb from each sentence (remember that the verb can sometimes be separable). Write down the infinitive of each verb.

Beispiel:

kommt ... an ⟶ ankommen

1 • Frau Geißler arbeitet für ein Fortbildungsinstitut in Mannheim.

2 • Am Montag fährt sie zu einer Konferenz nach Stuttgart.

3 • Ihr Zug fährt um 7 Uhr 15 ab.

4 • Dieser Zug ist ein Intercity, und sie steigt nicht um.

5 • Der Zug kommt um 11 Uhr 10 in Stuttgart an.

6 • Vom Bahnhof nimmt Frau Geißler ein Taxi zur Konferenz.

7 • Ihr Vortrag beginnt um 13 Uhr.

8 • Abends ist ein Empfang beim Rektor der Universität.

9 • Am nächsten Morgen hört Frau Geißler noch einen Vortrag von Prof. Meyer an.

10 • Dienstag mittag fährt sie wieder nach Mannheim.

Now that you know how to give instructions and directions in the imperative verb form, we will start using them alongside the English instructions later in this unit so you become more familiar with them.

B Here are some more instructions you will meet in the next few units, but the verbs are missing. Choose the correct verb from the box for each sentence. If there is a verb you are not familiar with, look it up in the glossary.

| sprechen | wählen | lesen | hören |
| ergänzen | arbeiten | schließen | schreiben |

Angebot der Woche

Rotkäppchen

deutscher Sekt

versch. Sorten

statt 3,57   1 Liter = 3,99 €

je 0,75 l **2,99 €**

1 • _____ Sie den Dialog!

2 • _____ Sie den Text!

3 • _____ Sie das Fenster!

4 • _____ Sie ein Fax!

5 • _____ Sie das richtige Wort!

6 • _____ Sie die Sätze!

7 • _____ Sie mit einem Partner.

8 • _____ Sie bitte langsamer.

UNIT **5**

2 Im Supermarkt

A Have a look at the departments of a typical supermarket and decide which items **a-x** opposite can be found in which department (in der…Abteilung).

1 • Wein

4 • Obst und Gemüse

2 • Fleisch

5 • Fisch

3 • Milchprodukte

6 • Fertiggerichte

a • die Pizza	**i** • das Joghurt	**q** • der Lachs
b • das Rumpsteak	**j** • das Müsli	**r** • der Schinken
c • das Schweinefilet	**k** • die Butter	**s** • die Pommes frites
d • der Brokkoli	**l** • die Orangen	**t** • der Weißkohl
e • die Bananen	**m** • der Rotwein	**u** • die Weintrauben
f • die Äpfel	**n** • das Bier	**v** • die Kartoffeln
g • die Krem	**o** • der Weißwein	**w** • die Bratwurst
h • der Käse	**p** • die Forelle	**x** • die gefrorenen Erbsen

LANGUAGE FOCUS

Plural of nouns

In the previous activity, a number of nouns were used in the plural.

The plural is usually formed by adding an ending to the singular form. Masculine and neuter nouns often take an **–e** in the plural, whereas feminine nouns often form the plural by adding **–n** or **–en**. The following rules will help you to form the plural:

Singular	Addition	Plural	Other examples
• Banane	–n	Bananen	Flaschen, Dosen, Erbsen, Tomaten, Weintrauben, Kartoffeln, Forellen, Orangen, Tassen
• Brot	–e	Brote	Salate, Stücke
• Packung	–en	Packungen	
• Glas	umlaut + –er	Gläser	Männer, Häuser
• Ei	–er	Eier	
• Waschmittel	–	Waschmittel	Fleisch, Würstchen, Käse, Schinken
• Joghurt	–s	Joghurts	Schampoos

Im Restaurant

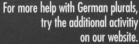

B **Hören Sie mal!**

Listen to the announcements and pick from the list below the articles on special offer this week.

> Danone-Joghurt
> Ariel-Waschmittel
> Holsteinisches Rindfleisch
> Becks-Bier im Sechser-Pack
> Melitta Kaffee
> Schwarzkopf-Schampoos
> Irische Butter
> Edamer Käse

C **Hören Sie nochmal!**

Listen to the announcements again and try to identify the prices of the following articles:

Artikel	Preis
1 Holsteiner Rindfleisch	
2 Schwarzwälder Räucherschinken	
3 Landliebe-Joghurt	
4 Schwarzkopf-Schampoos	

3 Ein bisschen Mathematik

A  Fragen Sie Ihren Partner. *Ask your partner.*
Wählen Sie Artikel von der Liste auf Seite 65.

Wieviel kostet ...?

1 • drei Kilo Rindfleisch

2 • zwei Flaschen Schampoo

3 • 300g Schinken

4 • Gläser Joghurt

Können Sie noch mehr Aufgaben machen?
Can you come up with additional questions?

Go to www.accesslanguages.com
to learn more about German
shopping on the Internet.

B Ergänzen Sie die fehlenden Wörter. *Complete the missing words.*
Use the Language Focus box on page 68.

1 • Im Supermarkt gibt es heute vier (   ) Milch im Sonderangebot.

2 • Für eine Sachertorte brauchen Sie sechs Eier und ein (   ) Butter.

3 • Herr Kurz liebt Mischgemüse. Er kauft sechs (   ).

4 • Für die Party kauft Peter vier (   ) Rotwein und vier (   ) Weißwein.

5 • Es gibt 125 Gramm, 250 Gramm und 500 Gramm (   ) Joghurt.

6 • Parmesan-Käse ist besser im (   ).

7 • „Sechs (   ) Schinken, bitte."

8 • Die Kinder kaufen eine (   ) Wiener Würstchen für die Party.

Im Restaurant

LANGUAGE FOCUS

Measurements/Measures

When you use quantities in German, you do not need an *of* construction as in English. You simply use the measure or measurement with the singular item that you are quantifying:

100g (Gramm) Käse	*100g of cheese*
250g (Gramm) Leberwurst	*250g of liver paté*
1l (Liter) Milch	*a litre of milk*
eine Flasche Rotwein	*a bottle of red wine*
drei Flaschen Bier	*three bottles of beer*
eine Packung Wiener Würstchen	*a packet of small Frankfurter-type sausages*
ein Stück Butter	*a pack of butter*
eine Scheibe Parmaschinken	*a slice of parma ham*
eine Dose Mischgemüse	*a tin of mixed veg (typically peas, carrots, cauliflower)*

Note that if you are using a plural, then only the quantifier takes the plural, not the actual item:

eine Flasch**e** Rotwein ⟶ sechs Flasch**en** Rotwein

```
F L R A N A N A S D L E R L O H A M B U R G E R T X F R
L S D O R A N G E N S A F T S D F L G R E B I E R P P O
R O T W E I N G B T T O D R R I S O T T O P O R S R A D
S E F S C H I N K E N S D L E S J O G H U R T T H G B Z
D S E S V A N I L L E E I S D K S E L S M U S C H E L N
E W Ü R S T C H E N S K E S P A R G E L C L D R J T F O
P A R M A S C H I N K E N S E N K A R T O F F E L N N A
D E R T S H A U P T G E R I C H T G O Y E J D Ü R S F B
S E L S L B R O T F E R L F S U P P E F W A S S E R T F
F F L E R Ü S C H O K O L A D E N K R E M E A U B O F C
```

4 Word search

🎲 ▶ Find as many food-related words in this puzzle as possible. The words are only written horizontally.

Look at the menu on page 69 for ideas!

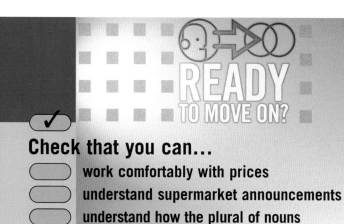

Check that you can...
- work comfortably with prices
- understand supermarket announcements
- understand how the plural of nouns is formed.

LEARNING TIP:

This unit is all about choosing and ordering food in a restaurant. As with many other countries, fast-food chains are on the increase in Germany and the German-speaking world. The instantly recognisable logos and comfortingly familiar menus can offer a 'home-from-home' haven to the weary traveller. The language is equally transferable:

Einen Cheeseburger und einen Vanille-Milkshake, bitte.

If travelling in Germany, your trip will be more interesting if you try some of the local cuisine. And local, in a city such as Berlin for example, does not necessarily mean traditional German cooking. Cuisine influenced by local ethnic communities, such as Greek, Turkish or Italian, is widely available.

5 Die Speisekarte

A Look at the menu below and try to work out what the following words are in German:

Rocket salad   Tomato soup   Main course   Asparagus
Beef steak

Café Orange
Speisekarte

Vorspeisen

Rukolasalat mit Parmesan	€6,00
Salat von Jacobsmuscheln und Endivien	€8,00
Tomatensuppe	€5.50
Auberginenpüree mit Pittabrot	€5,00

Hauptgerichte

Spargel mit Parmaschinken, neuen Kartoffeln und Sauce Hollandaise	€9,00
Hähnchenbrustfilet mit Pommes frites und Erbsen	€9,50
Heilbuttsteak mit Reis und Buttersauce	€10,50
Rindersteak mit Pommes frites und Waldpilzen	€13,00

Desserts

Schokoladenkrem	€4,00
Vanilleeis mit heißen Himbeeren	€4,50
Apfelstrudel mit warmer Vanillesauce	€3,00

Getränke

Rotwein	Glas (0,2l)	Karaffe (0,5l)
Rioja DOC	€3,50	€7,50
Beaujolais AC	€3,50	€7,50
Côte de Bourgogne AC	€4,00	€8,50

Weißwein	Glas (0,2l)	Karaffe (0,5l)
Soave DOC Tesi	€3,00	€6,50
Morio Muskat QBA	€3,00	€6,50
Grüner Veltiner	€3,50	€7,00

Weizenbier	€2,50
Pilsner	€2,50
Orangensaft (frisch gepresst)	€3,00
Orangensaft	€2,00
Apfelsaft	€2,00
Limonade	€2,00
Fanta	€1,50
Coca Cola	€1,50

Im Restaurant UNIT 5

LANGUAGE FOCUS

If you would like something (from a menu or in a shop, for example), you need to put that object (the direct object) in a new case: the accusative case. The accusative case distinguishes the subject of a sentence from its direct object.

The accusative case in German causes changes to masculine articles, but not feminine or neuter articles:

subject	verb	direct object	
Mrs Turner	buys	a salmon	for dinner.

	definite articles		indefinite articles	
	nominative	accusative	nominative	accusative
(masc.)	der	**den**	ein	**einen**
(fem.)	die	die	eine	eine
(neut.)	das	das	ein	ein
(plur.)	die	die	–	–

	subject	verb	direct object
(masc.)	Peter	kauft	**einen** Lachs.
(fem.)	Meine Mutter	trinkt	eine Limonade.
(neut.)	Ich	kaufe	ein Auto.

B Hören Sie gut zu. Was bestellt Sophie? Lesen Sie noch einmal die Speisekarte in Übung A.

What does Sophie order? Read the menu in Exercise A again.

Our website offers more help on German cases.

6 Wer bestellt was?

A Üben Sie! Add endings where needed.

1 ein◯ Steak (*neut.*) mit Pommes frites (*plur.*), ein◯ Flasche (*fem.*) Bier

2 ein◯ Risotto (*masc.*), ein◯ Glas (*neut.*) Mineralwasser

3 ein◯ Schweinebraten (*masc.*), ein◯ Flasche (*fem.*) Wein

4 ein◯ Hamburger (*masc.*), Pommes Frites (*plur.*)

a **b** **c** **d**

B Welches Wort paßt? *Complete the sentences.*

| eine Flasche Weißwein | Pommes frites | einen Thunfischsalat | einen Orangensaft |
| Tomatensuppe | Steak (neut.) | vegetarische Hauptgerichte | eine Vorspeise |

1 • Für mich bitte keinen Wein. Ich möchte bitte ⟨_____⟩.

2 • Ich esse kein Fleisch. Haben Sie ⟨_____⟩?

3 • Die Suppe sieht gut aus. Ich möchte bitte einen Teller ⟨_____⟩ mit Brot.

4 • Wir möchten bitte ⟨_____⟩ und zwei Gläser.

5 • Ich möchte bitte keine ⟨_____⟩, sondern Reis zu meinem Steak.

6 • Möchten Sie ⟨_____⟩?

7 • Als Vorspeise möchte ich bitte ⟨_____⟩.

8 • Ich habe kein ⟨_____⟩ bestellt!

Im Restaurant

Many German restaurants have their own websites. For a selection of the best and ideas on how to use them to improve your German, go to www.accesslanguages.com

7 Kochen Sie gern?

A 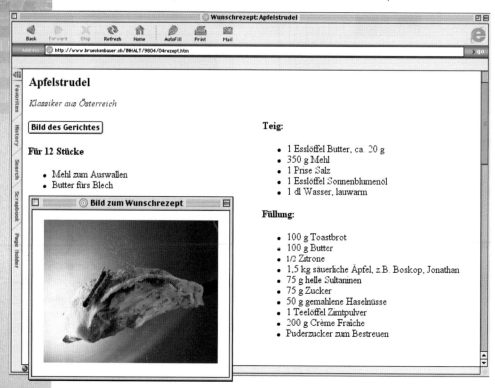 ⒶⒸ ▶ Viele Leute interessieren sich für das Kochen. Es gibt viele Kochbücher mit Rezepten und schönen Fotos. Hier ist ein Rezept aus dem Internet.

⊞ Wunschrezept: Apfelstrudel

Back | Forward | Stop | Refresh | Home | AutoFill | Print | Mail

Address: ⊕ http://www.brueckenbauer.ch/INHALT/9804/04rezept.htm › go

Apfelstrudel

Klassiker aus Österreich

[Bild des Gerichtes]

Für 12 Stücke

- Mehl zum Auswallen
- Butter fürs Blech

⊞ Bild zum Wunschrezept

Teig:

- 1 Esslöffel Butter, ca. 20 g
- 350 g Mehl
- 1 Prise Salz
- 1 Esslöffel Sonnenblumenöl
- 1 dl Wasser, lauwarm

Füllung:

- 100 g Toastbrot
- 100 g Butter
- 1/2 Zitrone
- 1,5 kg säuerliche Äpfel, z.B. Boskop, Jonathan
- 75 g helle Sultaninen
- 75 g Zucker
- 50 g gemahlene Haselnüsse
- 1 Teelöffel Zimtpulver
- 200 g Crème Fraîche
- Puderzucker zum Bestreuen

Welche Zutaten brauchen Sie **nicht** für das Rezept?
*Which ingredients do you **not** need for the recipe?*

> sugar   flour   currants   raisins   margarine   cinnamon
> vanilla   salt   ground hazelnuts   whipping cream   olive oil

Lesen Sie das Rezept noch einmal.
Was brauchen Sie? *What **do** you need?*

Ich brauche… *I need…*
The object is then in the accusative case.

- Für einen Apfelstrudel brauche ich:

B 🔊 ⚪ Was ist Ihr Lieblingsrezept? Backen Sie gern? Oder kochen Sie lieber? Machen Sie sich ein paar Notizen und dann erzählen Sie den anderen Studenten, was Ihr Lieblingsrezept ist.

Mein Lieblingsrezept ist …

Ich brauche …

LANGUAGE FOCUS

gern

To say that you like something, you need the word **gern**. This word can be used in conjunction with verbs and nouns to describe something you like doing, e.g.:

Ich koche gern.	*I like cooking.*
Ich gehe gern ins Theater.	*I like going to the theatre.*
Meine Mutter spielt gern Tennis.	*My mother likes playing tennis.*
Mein Sohn ißt gern Pizza.	*My son likes eating pizza.*
Mein Mann trinkt gern australischen Rotwein.	*My husband likes (drinking) Australian red wine.*
Viele Jungs spielen gern Fußball.	*Lots of boys like playing football.*

lieber

To express preference of one thing over another, the word **lieber** is used.

Ich esse lieber Reis (*as opposed to chips*).
Susanne spielt lieber Tennis (*as opposed to football*).
Wir fahren lieber mit dem Zug (*as opposed to by car*).

The words **gern** and **lieber** go after the verb in the sentence.

Im Restaurant

8 Im Restaurant

A Hören Sie den Dialog. Then put the pictures in the right order.

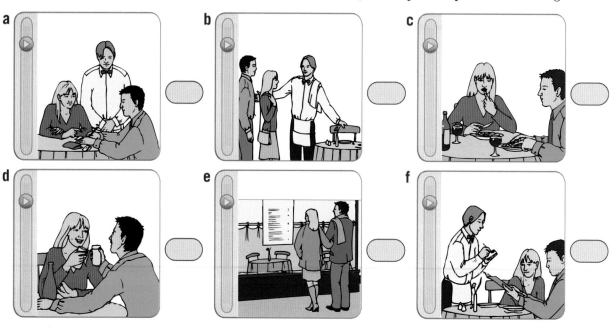

B Hören Sie gut zu. Was sagt der Kellner, was sagt Stefan, und was sagt Claudia?

Listen carefully and tick who says what.

		Kellner	Stefan	Claudia
1	Ja, einen Tisch für zwei Personen.			
2	Was möchten Sie trinken?			
3	Ich möchte bitte ein Mineralwasser.			
4	Ich hätte gern die Lachspastete als Vorspeise.			
5	Haben Sie schon gewählt?			
6	Und ich möchte bitte die kalte Erbsensuppe und dann das Filetsteak.			
7	Möchtest du ein Dessert?			
8	Könnten wir vielleicht ein paar Oliven zum Knabbern haben?			
9	Und vielleicht einen Wein zum Essen?			
10	Ja, einen Roten bitte.			

C  Schüttelkasten.

> | Haben Sie | den Krabbensalat. | bitte. | Ich möchte bitte |
> | einen Risotto | Sie, bitte? | Pommes frites. |
> | schon gewählt? | Frau Neumann bestellt | Ein Glas |
> | Was möchten | Haben Sie | einen australischen |
> | möchte ich | die Weinkarte. | Weizenbier, | als Hauptgericht. |
> | Für mich bitte keine | Als Vorspeise | Pinot grigio? |

To get you started, here are some English examples made up from the words in the Schüttelkasten above:

* No chips for me, please.
* I would like the wine menu, please.
* Frau Neumann orders a risotto as a main course.

How many sentences can you make?

D Was möchten Sie, bitte?

Arbeiten Sie mit einem Partner. Sie sind Gast in einem Restaurant und Ihr Partner ist der Kellner oder die Kellnerin. Lesen Sie noch einmal die Speisekarte auf Seite 69 und wählen Sie eine Vorspeise, ein Hauptgericht, ein Dessert und etwas zu trinken.

When you have finished, swap roles with your partner.

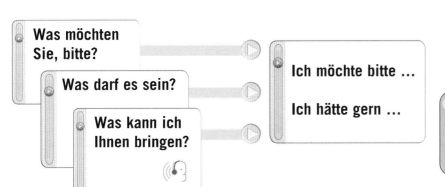

Was möchten Sie, bitte?

Was darf es sein?

Was kann ich Ihnen bringen?

Ich möchte bitte …

Ich hätte gern …

LEARNING TIP:
Don't forget to put the items you are ordering from the waiter into the accusative case!

Im Restaurant UNIT 5

9 Ein Spiel zum Lernen und für die Konzentration!

 Das ist ein Spiel für die ganze Gruppe. Ein Student beginnt:

Meine Mutter geht zum Supermarkt und kauft …

… drei Flaschen Milch.

Der nächste Student macht weiter:

Meine Mutter geht zum Supermarkt und kauft drei Flaschen Milch und ein Brot.

Der nächste Student sagt:

Meine Mutter geht zum Supermarkt und kauft drei Flaschen Milch, ein Brot und 500g Würstchen …

Wie weit kommen Sie?

10 Der Restaurantführer

Ein Restaurantführer gibt Informationen über Restaurants in einer Region oder einem Land. Lesen Sie hier über einige Restaurants in Berlin. Dann beantworten Sie bitte die Fragen auf der nächsten Seite.

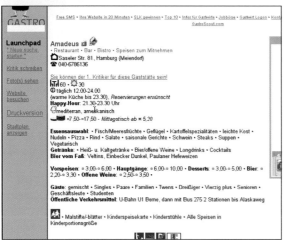

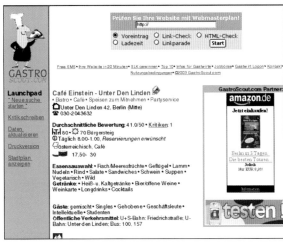

Bitte beantworten Sie diese Fragen auf englisch:

1 • Which restaurant has conference facilities for 30 participants?

2 • Which restaurant is closed on Sundays?

3 • Which restaurant has a catering service?

4 • Which new restaurant serves German food?

5 • Where can you eat Mexican food?

6 • Which restaurant does not serve food on Mondays?

7 • Which restaurants serve draught beer?

8 • Which restaurant is suitable for families?

Im Restaurant UNIT 5

11 Noch ein Restaurantbesuch

Claudia und Stefan sind im Restaurant.
They have finished their meal and would like to pay now.

A Hören Sie den Dialog und beantworten Sie dann die Fragen auf Deutsch:

1 • Wer bezahlt die Rechnung?
2 • Was kostet der Rotwein?

3 • Was kostet Claudias Essen?
4 • Was kostet Stefans Essen?

B Beschreiben Sie auf Englisch, warum Claudia und Stefan einen Grappa auf Kosten des Hauses bekommen.

12 Sie sind dran!

Arbeiten Sie mit zwei Partnern. Sie brauchen: einen Kellner oder eine Kellnerin und zwei Gäste.

Wählen Sie von der Speisekarte auf Seite 69 etwas zu essen und zu trinken. Bestellen Sie dann beim 'Kellner' und fragen Sie am Ende bitte nach der Rechnung. *Choose something from the menu on page 69 and ask for the bill at the end.*

GLOSSARY

Nouns

Apfel (m)	apple
Apfelstrudel (m)	apple strudel
Aubergine (f)	aubergine
Banane (f)	banana
Bier (n)	beer
Bratwurst (f)	sausages (fried, rather than Frankfurter type)
Brokkoli (m)	broccoli
Brust (f)	breast
Butter (f)	butter
Dessert (n)	dessert

GLOSSARY

German	English	German	English
Dose (f)	tin	**Nachspeise** (f)	dessert
Empfang (m)	reception	**Obst** (n)	fruit
Erbse (f)	pea	**Olive** (f)	olive
Fenster (n)	window	**Orange** (f)	orange
Fertiggericht (n)	convenience meal	**Orangensaft** (m)	orange juice
Fisch (m)	fish	**Packung** (f)	pack
Flasche (f)	bottle	**Pommes frites** (pl)	French fries
Fleisch (n)	meat	**Räucherschinken** (m)	dry-cured ham
Forelle (f)	trout	**Reis** (m)	rice
Fortbildungsinstitut (n)	training provider	**Rezept** (n)	recipe
		Risotto (m)	risotto
Gemüse (n)	vegetables	**Rotwein** (m)	red wine
Haarwaschmittel (n)	shampoo	**Rumpsteak** (n)	rump steak
Hähnchen (n)	chicken	**Sahne** (f)	cream (as in double, single)
Hauptgericht (n)	main course	**Satz** (m)	sentence
Himbeere (f)	raspberry	**Scheibe** (f)	slice
Jakobsmuschel (f)	scallop	**Schinken** (m)	ham
Joghurt (m)	yoghurt	**Schokoladenkrem** (n)	chocolate mousse
Kartoffel (f)	potato		
Käse (m)	cheese	**Schweinebraten** (m)	roast pork
Kellner (m)	waiter (male)	**Schweinefilet** (n)	pork fillet
Kellnerin (f)	waitress	**Spargel** (m)	asparagus
Konferenz (f)	conference	**Speisekarte** (f)	menu
Krabbe (f)	prawn	**Stück** (n)	piece
Krem (f)	cream (face cream or *crème* as in *crème fraîche* or mousse)	**Suppe** (f)	soup
		Tisch (m)	table
		Vanilleeis (n)	vanilla ice-cream
Lachs (m)	salmon	**Vorspeise** (f)	first course
Limonade (f)	lemonade	**Vortrag** (m)	lecture
Milchprodukt (n)	dairy product	**Waschmittel** (n)	washing powder
Mineralwasser (n)	mineral water	**Wein (m)**	wine
Müsli (n)	muesli	**Weintrauben**	grapes

Im Restaurant

GLOSSARY

Weißkohl (m)	(white) cabbage	fragen	to ask
Weißwein (m)	white wine	hören	to hear, to listen
Weizenbier (n)	wheat beer	kochen	to cook
		kosten	to cost
Adjectives		schließen	to close
langsam	slow	schreiben	to write
neu	new	sich interessieren für	to be interested in
		trinken	to drink
Verbs		wählen	to choose
backen	to bake		
bestellen	to order	**Prepositions**	
ergänzen	to complete	mit	with
essen	to eat		

LOOKING FORWARD

In Unit 6, you will learn more about travelling to Germany. The holiday-planning website below allows a very detailed and personalised search for the holiday destination of your dreams. Look at the categories and decide on at least ten criteria necessary for your dream holiday.

UNIT 6
Unterwegs in Deutschland

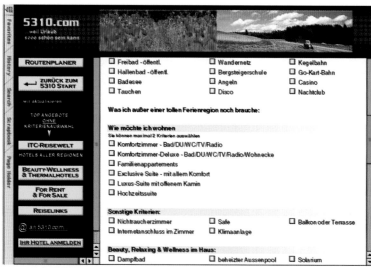

UNIT 6
Unterwegs in Deutschland

By the end of this unit you will be able to:

- Book a holiday
- Describe a holiday destination
- Find out how to get around in Germany
- Describe your symptoms to a doctor
- Understand instructions from a chemist
- Use a certain type of preposition
- Use modal verbs correctly

1 Wissen Sie noch?

A ✎ ◌ Kriterien für die Urlaubsplanung.

In Unit 5, we looked at a number of criteria for planning a holiday. Can you remember five of them?

1 • Saison   **3** • ⬭   **5** • ⬭   **7** • ⬭

2 • Zielort   **4** • ⬭   **6** • ⬭

UNIT **6**

B Ergänzen Sie bitte die Pluralendungen.

1 • drei Flasche( ) Rotwein

2 • zwei Packung( ) Oliven

3 • sechs Scheib( ) Parmaschinken

4 • zwei Rolle( ) Papier

5 • zehn Flasche( ) Limonade

6 • vier Dose( ) Cola

7 • sechs Gläs( ) Joghurt

8 • zwanzig Dose( ) Bier

C Ergänzen Sie die Artikel. Beachten Sie, daß Sie **der**, **ein** und
kein für maskuline Wörter verändern müssen.

Frau Müller kocht gern. Am Samstag gibt sie ein( )
Dinnerparty. Sie lädt ein( ) Freundin, ein( )
Freund und ein( ) befreundetes Ehepaar ein. Sie
bittet ihren Mann, d( ) Wein zu kaufen. Sie sagt:
„Vergiss nicht, Marianne trinkt kein( ) Rosé. Vielleicht
kannst du auch ein( ) guten Prosecco mitbringen?"

Dann geht Frau Müller einkaufen. Als Vorspeise plant sie
Parmaschinken mit Melone. 'Ich frage d( )
Fleischer, ob er d( ) Schinken ganz dünn schneiden
kann', denkt sie.

Als Hauptgericht sucht sie ein( ) schönen, frischen
Lachs aus. Sie plant ein( ) leichtes, sommerliches
Fischessen. Als Dessert möchte sie ein( )
Schokoladenkuchen backen.

2 Urlaubszeit

Barbara und Ingo wollen im August nach Bayern fahren.
Sie brauchen einen Urlaub!

Viele neue Wörter – keine Panik! Hier sind ein paar
Schlüsselwörter.

Schlüsselwörter

zur Abwechslung	*for a change*
Ferienwohnung (f)	*holiday apartment*
verreisen	*to go away/travel*
buchen	*to book*

A Hören Sie den Dialog und entscheiden Sie, wer was sagt.

	Barbara	Ingo

1 • Wie wäre es mit Italien?

2 • Wir können ja mal nach Rügen fahren.

3 • Vielleicht können wir eine kleine Ferienwohnung mieten?

4 • Wieviele Zimmer brauchen wir denn?

5 • Katja war dort schon mal im Urlaub.

6 • Die Kinder können dann ein separates Zimmer haben.

7 • Ich möchte dieses Jahr mindestens zwei Wochen verreisen.

8 • Ich sehe heute Abend mal nach.

B Hören Sie den Dialog noch einmal und entscheiden Sie, ob
die richtige Antwort **a**, **b** oder **c** ist.

1 • Which holiday destination is first
suggested by Ingo?
  a Paris
  b Tuscany
  c Bavaria

2 • Which holiday destination do they
decide on?
  a Bavaria
  b Riga
  c an island in Germany

3 • What kind of accommodation are they
looking for?
  a two-bedroom apartment
  b one-bedroom apartment
  c camping

4 • How are they hoping to find suitable
accommodation?
  a through friends
  b through a specialised website
  c through adverts

5 • Who has been to the destination before?
  a a friend of theirs
  b Ingo
  c Barbara

6 • What is special about the island?
  a The islanders speak their own
language.
  b There are no cars on the island.
  c There are few people on the island.

www.accesslanguages.com **has links**
to interesting German holiday sites.

C Hören Sie den Dialog noch einmal und ergänzen Sie die Lücken *(gaps)*.

1 • Wo wollen wir denn im August (   )?

2 • Wie wäre es denn zur Abwechslung mit einem (   ) in Deutschland?

3 • Wir können ja nach Rügen (   ).

4 • Vielleicht können wir eine kleine (   ) mieten.

5 • Man kann im Internet nach verschiedenen (   ) recherchieren.

6 • Die meisten Ferienwohnungen haben ein großes Zimmer – halb (   ) und halb (   ).

7 • Die Ferienwohnung darf nicht zu (   ) und nicht zu (   ) sein.

There are a number of options in German to express the notion of going *to* a place. Which one you choose will depend on whether the place in question is a town/country, a region, a place by the sea, etc.

Wir fahren ...

Country, town, city:	**nach** Spanien, **nach** London, **nach** Stafford, **nach** Cornwall
Place in the mountains:	**in** die Alpen, **in** die Dolomiten, **in** die Rocky Mountains
Place by the water:	**an** die Ostsee, **an** das Schwarze Meer, **an** den Nil
Region:	**in** den Lake District, **in** die Berge, **in** den Schwarzwald

Note that in conjunction with the prepositions **in** and **an**, you need to use the accusative case:
an de**n** Nil, in de**n** Schwarzwald.
Remember that only masculine articles are affected by this change.

An introduction to prepositions

In the previous activity, you met two prepositions: **in** and **an**. Here they were used with the meaning: *by* and *into*. Prepositions are notoriously difficult to translate literally, however, so it is advisable to memorise them in context.

Other prepositions that take the accusative case are:

durch	*through*	ohne	*without*
für	*for*	um	*around*
gegen	*against*	entlang	*along*

Remember the changes to masculine words in the accusative case:

masculine	feminine	neuter	plural
den	die	das	die
einen	eine	ein	–
meinen	meine	mein	meine

D  Sie sind dran!
Arbeiten Sie in einer kleinen Gruppe. Wohin fahren Ihre Partner in den Urlaub?

Partner A
Wohin fahren Sie in den Urlaub?

Partner B
Ich fahre nach ...
in die.../das.../den...
an die .../das.../den...

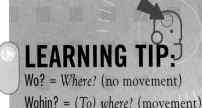

LEARNING TIP:
Wo? = *Where?* (no movement)
Wohin? = *(To) where?* (movement)

ACCESS GERMAN

3 Üben Sie!

Ergänzen Sie bitte die Endungen in dem Brief von Leila.
Are the words masculine, feminine or neuter?

Vielank, den 25. Mai 2003

Liebe Oma,

Jetzt bin ich schon eine Woche auf dem Reiterhof. Es ist ganz toll hier! Ich reite jeden Morgen für ein(   ) Stunde. Meine Freundin Sabrina kommt auch mit. Manchmal reiten wir durch d(   ) Wald und manchmal durch d(   ) Ort. Der Ort heißt Vielank und ist sehr klein. Man kann in zwei Minuten um d(   ) Ort laufen! Das ist schon anders als in Berlin! Am besten sind die Pferde hier. Mein Pferd heißt Silberpfeil. Ich möchte gar nicht mehr ohne mein(   ) Pferd sein! Schade, daß du nicht sehen kannst, wie ich durch d(   ) Ort und d(   ) Fluß entlang reite. Am Sonntag fahre ich wieder nach Hause. Dann rufe ich dich an.

Ganz liebe Grüße,

Deine Leila

Practise your German genders on our website.

4 Welche ist Ihre Trauminsel?

In dem folgenden Text können Sie viele interessante Informationen über die Ostseeinseln Rügen und Hiddensee lesen. Bevor Sie den Text lesen, erraten Sie den Titel.

Tipp: Der Titel hat vier Wörter.

auelUrlaTrnubaufmderis

Lösung: Url(   ) (   ) (   )   Tr(   )

LEARNING TIP:
The text on the next page is authentic which means that a number of words will be unfamiliar. This activity will help you to get the idea of reading for gist rather than in detail. Don't worry if you don't understand whole phrases, sentences or individual words. Concentrate on getting the overall meaning of the text.

A Lesen Sie den Text auf der nächsten Seite und entscheiden Sie, ob die Sätze 1 bis 8 richtig oder falsch sind.

Mecklenburg-Vorpommerns Inselwelt

Die Halbinsel Rügen, über den Rügendamm von Stralsund zu erreichen, ist perfekt für einen Traumurlaub: ein Paradies für Naturfreunde, Vogelliebhaber und Angler. Jedes Jahr kann man Kormorane sehen, wie sie in den abgestorbenen Bäumen der Halbinsel hocken. Die 2500 schwarzen Vögel sind ein dramatischer Anblick. Für die Fischer sind die Kormorane allerdings ein Problem, weil sie mehr und mehr Heringe aus dem Meer fischen.

Aber auch Kunstfreunde können auf Rügen auf ihre Kosten kommen. Am Kap Arkona gibt es einen Theater- und Musiksommer, und in Zinnowitz eine Reihe von Kunstaustellungen und Konzerten.

Westlich von Rügen liegt die Insel Hiddensee. Hiddensee ist dafür berühmt, daß es dort keine Autos gibt. Dafür kann man auf Hiddensee mit dem Fahrrad fahren oder manchmal auch mit traditionellen Pferdekutschen durch die wunderschönen Alleen, die schon hundert Jahre alt sind.

Die Inselwelt von Mecklenburg-Vorpommern hat für jeden etwas zu bieten: spektakuläre Naturschauspiele, Kultur, Landschaft und Sport. Versuchen Sie es selbst – unter 03838/80770 bekommen Sie weitere Informationen.

	Richtig	Falsch
1 • There is reduced access to Rügen by car.		
2 • The cormorants present a huge problem for the fishermen.		
3 • Rügen is particularly attractive for nature lovers.		
4 • There are no cars on Hiddensee.		
5 • There is a theatre festival in Zinnowitz.		
6 • The trees lining the roads are two hundred years old.		
7 • A traditional means of transport on Hiddensee are horse-drawn carriages.		
8 • There are also opportunities for sports lovers.		

Unterwegs in Deutschland UNIT 6

B 🅰️🅲️ ✏️ 🔊 Lesen Sie den Text noch einmal und schreiben Sie dann die richtigen Wörter in die Lücken.

spektakuläre Naturschauspiele
Kunstausstellungen
Konzerte
Autos
wunderschönen Alleen
Urlaubsparadies
bieten
Fahrrad

Rügen ist ein ⬭. Rügen hat für jeden etwas zu ⬭. Die ⬭ ⬭ sind schon hundert Jahre alt. Das beste an Hiddensee ist, daß es keine ⬭ gibt. Aber man kann mit dem ⬭ durch die Alleen fahren oder auch schwimmen. Man kann dabei ⬭ sehen. Auch für Kulturfreunde gibt es viel Gutes auf Rügen: ⬭ und ⬭.

C ✏️ 🔊 Schreiben Sie jetzt einen kleinen Werbetext über einen Urlaubsort in England für einen Kollegen in Deutschland.

5 Wohin fahren Sie?

 Hier sehen Sie einen Fragebogen (*questionnaire*) von der Urlaubswebseite. Arbeiten Sie mit einem Partner und füllen Sie ihn zusammen aus. Ask each other questions.

READY TO MOVE ON?

✓

Check that you can...

- work comfortably with the prepositions introduced in this unit which take the accusative
- say where you are going on holiday
- understand more complex information about holiday destinations.

6 Was kann man auf Rügen machen?

LANGUAGE FOCUS

The German word **man** is often translated as *one* in English, but it does not have the same old-fashioned resonance. **Man** is very commonly used and is closer to the English *you*.

When using **man**, the verb needs to be in the third person singular (*he/she* form) e.g.:

In England fährt man auf der linken Seite.
In England, you drive on the left-hand side.

In Übung 4 haben Sie viele Informationen über Rügen gelesen. Formulieren Sie jetzt Sätze. Was kann man wo machen?

Arbeiten Sie mit einem Partner. Fragen Sie Ihren Partner: Was kann man wo machen?

Man kann	auf Rügen	in Galerien gehen.
	in Griechenland	gut essen.
	in London	gut wandern.
	im Schwarzwald	schwimmen.
		Radfahren.
		Sehenswürdigkeiten besichtigen.
		die Queen sehen.
		Kuckucksuhren kaufen.
		frischen Fisch essen.
		surfen.
		in berühmte Clubs gehen.

Machen Sie noch ein paar Sätze.

- In New York ...
- In Venedig ...
- Im Lake District ...

B Hören Sie jetzt den Dialog und wählen Sie dann die Symptome, die der kleine Junge hat.

Kopfschmerzen   Fieber   Durchfall

Bauchschmerzen   Migräne   Verstopfung

Zahnschmerzen   Ohrenschmerzen   Nasenbluten

C Hören Sie jetzt den Dialog noch einmal und entscheiden Sie, ob diese Sätze richtig oder falsch sind.

	Richtig	Falsch
1 • Karl's father is not well.		
2 • He has a high temperature.		
3 • The young son is ill.		
4 • His mother is going to ring the doctor.		
5 • The child has a very high temperature.		
6 • Ingo suggests a cold compress on his forehead.		
7 • The mother has put cold compresses round his leg.		
8 • Ingo has telephoned a doctor.		

D Hören Sie den Dialog noch einmal und verbinden Sie dann die korrekten Satzteile.

1	Der Karl hat	können Sie Paracetamol nehmen.
2	Er hat auch	ob das Fieber jetzt zurück geht.
3	Mach doch erst mal	das Fieber runter.
4	Vielleicht sollten wir	ganz hohes Fieber.
5	Hoffentlich geht	solche Sorgen!
6	Gegen Kopfschmerzen	einen Arzt anrufen?
7	Warte doch erst einmal,	ein nasses Tuch auf die Stirn.
8	Ich mache mir	ganz schlimme Kopfschmerzen.

UNIT 6

9 Können Sie helfen?

A C Diese Leute sind krank. Was sollten sie tun?

1

Bauchschmerzen: Kamillentee trinken, eine Wärmflasche auf den Bauch legen

2

hohes Fieber: viel trinken, viel schlafen, Paracetamol nehmen

3

Zahnschmerzen: zum Zahnarzt gehen

4

Migräne, schlimme Kopfschmerzen: im Bett oder auf dem Sofa liegen, Wasser trinken, schlafen, zum Arzt gehen

10 Wer ist der richtige Arzt?

Dr. Bernd Wagner
Internist

Dr. Kathrin Wegener
Frauenärztin

Dr. Sabine Fischer
Hautärztin

Dr. med. Johannes Berger
Facharzt für HNO

Peter Scholze
Zahnarzt

Dr. med. Patrick Kietzer
Facharzt für Neurologie

Joshua Rosenburg
Chiropraktiker

A Schreiben Sie den Namen neben den entsprechenden Fachbereich.

paediatrician

ear, nose and throat (ENT) specialist

chiropractor

Dr. Kira Barthels
FÄ für Orthopädie

urologist

dentist

Dr. Ayshe Kienast
Kinderärztin

neurologist

specialist for internal complaints

Prof. Dr. B. Wericke
Facharzt für Urologie

dentist

dermatologist

specialist for orthopaedic complaints

B Sie sind dran!

Arbeiten Sie mit einem Partner.

Beispiel:

(A) **Ich habe Ohrenschmerzen.**

(B) **Gehen Sie zu einem Hals-, Nasen-, Ohrenarzt.**

Ich habe Bauchschmerzen.
Ich habe Rückenschmerzen.
Ich habe einen Hautausschlag.
Ich kann nicht mehr gut lesen.
Ich habe starke Halsschmerzen.
Ich habe ständig Kopfschmerzen.

Gehen Sie zu einem ...

UNIT 6

97

11 Holistische Medizin

Sehen Sie sich bitte das folgende Bild an. Was, glauben Sie, kann man auf dieser Webseite finden?

Informationen zum Thema

Diskutieren Sie die Informationen. Hier sind ein paar Vokabeln:

Das (　　　) oder (　　　) sieht

interessant	aus.
langweilig	
neu	
merkwürdig	
unbekannt	
informativ	

Gibt es (　　　) auch in England? Essen Sie Naturprodukte?

Naturprodukte sind

teuer.
(nicht) besser.
schadstoffarm.

Schmecken Naturprodukte besser oder nicht?

GLOSSARY

Nouns

Anblick (m)	view
Auge (n)	eye
Bauch (m)	stomach, belly
Bein (n)	leg
Ellenbogen (m)	elbow
Elternabend (m)	parents' evening
Fahrrad (n)	bicycle
Ferienwohnung (f)	holiday apartment
Fluß (m)	river
Fuß (m)	foot
Geburtstagskuchen (m)	birthday cake
Halbinsel (f)	peninsula
Jahr (n)	year
Kneipe (f)	pub
Kormoran (m)	cormorant
Meer (n)	sea
Minute (f)	minute
Morgen (m)	morning
Nase (f)	nose
Naturfreund (m)	nature lover
Ohr (n)	ear
Ort (m)	place, village
Paradies (n)	paradise
Pfannkuchen (m)	pancake
Pferd (m)	horse
Reihe (f)	row, series
Reiterhof (m)	holiday destination that offers horse-riding holidays

Rolle (f)	role
Schulter (f)	shoulder
Sehenswürdigkeit (f)	sight
Sorge (f)	worry
Stunde (f)	hour
Urlaub (m)	holiday
Vogelliebhaber (m)	bird watcher
Wald (m)	woods
Zielort (m)	destination

Adjectives

abgestorben	dead (here: trees)
folgend	following
krank	ill
langweilig	boring
merkwürdig	strange
perfekt	perfect
spektakulär	spectacular
toll	great (colloquial)
unbekannt	unknown
weiter	further

Verbs

besichtigen	to visit
einladen	to invite
erraten	to guess
erreichen	to reach
mieten	to hire, to rent
nachsehen	to check
recherchieren	to research
verreisen	to travel
wandern	to walk

Unterwegs in Deutschland UNIT

6

GLOSSARY

Adverbs

hoffentlich	hopefully
unbedingt	definitively

Prepositions

an	to, at
in	in

Phrases

auf ihre Kosten kommen	will get their money's worth
(ganz) liebe Grüße	lots of love (to end a letter)
nach Hause	(to go) home
zur Abwechslung	for a change

LOOKING AHEAD

EDEN
Jeden Tag gesund genießen.

Winterfit in 6 Tagen

Cevita

NEU! Ein köstliches Frucht-Gemüse-Getränk zur Stärkung des Immunsystems: Trinken Sie sich winterfit mit EDEN Cevita! Am besten mit dem 6-Tage-Paket – einfach täglich eine Flasche heiß oder kalt genießen.

Nur im 6-Tage-Paket:
Wellnessplan und Aromaöl

Exklusiv in Ihrem Reformhaus

UNIT 7
Beim Arzt

In Unit 7, you will learn about pharmacies in Germany and how to understand common medication.

Read this advert. What does the product promise?

UNIT 7
Beim Arzt

> **By the end of this unit you will be able to:**
> - Arrange an appointment at the doctor's
> - Use another grammatical case (the dative)
> - Use a certain type of preposition
> - Express dissatisfaction
> - Express your opinion and discuss it with others

We suggest that you come back to this checklist as you progress through the unit. You can then judge how you are getting on.

1 Wissen Sie noch?

A))) Wie geht es Ihnen?

How would you say in German that:

1 • You have a stomach ache?

2 • Your husband has a headache?

3 • Your daughter has a temperature?

4 • You have a skin complaint?

5 • Your son has toothache?

6 • You have backache?

B  Wohin fahren Sie?

Which preposition?

1 • Dieses Jahr fahren wir ( ) das Schwarze Meer.

2 • Zum Geburtstag schenkt mein Mann mir eine Reise ( ) Paris.

3 • Wollen wir einen Ausflug ( ) Leipzig machen?

4 • Meine Tochter fährt mit ihrem Freund ( ) Dolomiten.

5 • Am liebsten fahre ich im Urlaub ( ) die Berge.

6 • Kennen Sie Schottland? Sie sollten unbedingt einmal ( ) Edinburgh fahren.

7 • Wir haben einen kleinen Bungalow in Prerow. Deshalb fahren wir im Sommer jedes Wochenende ( ) die Ostsee.

8 • Mein Traumurlaub wäre ein Trip ( ) Australien.

C Welches Modalverb?

Do you remember the modal verbs from Unit 6? How would you say the following in German?

1 • I cannot come to the cinema tonight (because I am working).

2 • I must not have any more wine (because I am driving).

3 • I should go to bed earlier during the week (because I am too tired).

4 • I should not have any more cheese (because I am on a diet).

5 • I have to go at 7.30 (because I am catching a train).

6 • I need another six stamps in the set (and then I have the complete set).

2 Beim Arzt

On a trip to Germany, Alison has developed a bad cold. Her temperature is not going down, so she has decided to consult a doctor.

A Have a look at these practice signs, then answer the following question.

Welchen Arzt ruft Alison an?

B Hören Sie das Telefongespräch an, und beantworten Sie dann die Fragen auf Englisch.

1. • How long has Alison been feeling unwell?

2. • What are her symptoms?

3. • Where is Alison staying?

4. • What is Dr Kaddatz doing between 12 and 2 p.m.?

5. • What time can Alison see Dr Kaddatz?

6. • What form does the receptionist ask Alison to bring along?

7. • Where did she get the form?

C 🎧 ✏️ ▷ Hören Sie das Gespräch noch einmal an, und wählen Sie dann das korrekte Wort.

> **Hausbesuche** **dann** **kommen** **Formular**
> **Termin** **Fieber** **Patientin** **Reise**

1 • Sind Sie eine ⬭⬭⬭⬭⬭⬭ von Dr. Kaddatz?

2 • Kann ich bitte einen ⬭⬭⬭⬭⬭⬭ mit Dr. Kaddatz haben?

3 • Ich habe seit einer Woche hohes ⬭⬭⬭⬭⬭⬭.

4 • Über Mittag macht der Doktor ⬭⬭⬭⬭⬭⬭.

5 • Könnten Sie kurz nach 15 Uhr ⬭⬭⬭⬭⬭⬭?

6 • Haben Sie ein E111-⬭⬭⬭⬭⬭⬭?

7 • Bis ⬭⬭⬭⬭⬭⬭, Frau Simpson.

8 • Das Formular habe ich mir vor meiner ⬭⬭⬭⬭⬭⬭ geholt.

D 🗣️ 👥 ▷ Hören Sie den Dialog noch einmal an. Arbeiten Sie dann mit einem Partner: Sie sind Patient, und Ihr Partner arbeitet bei einem Arzt. Machen Sie bitte einen Termin.

appointment for toothache 🗣️	sorry – no appointment 🎧
bad toothache 🗣️	Are you a patient? 🎧
No, but very bad pain. 🗣️	appointment at 4 p.m. this afternoon

3 Was ist die richtige Medizin?

These remedies are available over the counter at the chemist's in Germany. The instructions for certain complaints have been taken from the packages.

Fragen Sie Ihren Partner:

1 • Welches Medikament hilft bei Kopfschmerzen?

2 • Wie viele Aspirin darf ich nehmen?

3 • Hilft Kwai gegen Fieber?

4 • Wie oft muß ich Kwai nehmen?

5 • Was hilft bei Schmerzen?

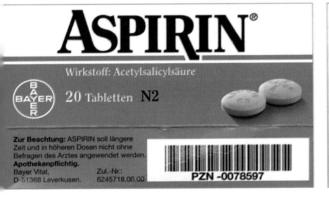

Zusammensetzung: Eine Tablette enthält 500mg Acetylsalicylsäure.
Anwendung: Leichte bis mäßig starke Schmerzen, Fieber.
Dosierung: Soweit nicht anders verordnet, nehmen Jugendliche und Erwachsene ein bis zwei Tabletten. Tagesdosis bis sechs Tabletten.

Wirkstoff: Trockenpulver aus Allium sativum (Knoblauchzwiebel).
Anwendung: Hoher Wirkstoffgehalt vorbeugend gegen allgemeine Arterienverkalkung (allgemeine Arteriosklerose).
Dosierung: Soweit nicht anders verordnet, drei mal täglich drei Dragees mit etwas Flüssigkeit zu den Mahlzeiten einnehmen.

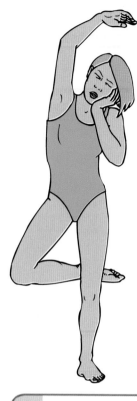

4 Üben Sie

 For this game the imperative of verbs is used again. If you need a reminder, see page 180.

Arbeiten Sie mit drei oder vier Partnern. Schreiben Sie auf ein Stück Papier eine medizinische Beschwerde und auf ein anderes Stück Papier eine Empfehlung. Dann mischen Sie alle Papierstücke und legen die Beschwerden auf die eine Seite und die Empfehlungen auf die andere Seite.

Beispiel:

Beschwerde:

Ich habe Kopfschmerzen.

Empfehlung:

Trinken Sie weniger Kaffee.

The aim of the game is to pair up as many complaints and pieces of advice as possible. They do not all have to be too serious!

Beschwerde:

- schwere Beine
- Bauchschmerzen
- Rückenschmerzen
- kann nachts nicht schlafen
- Zahnschmerzen
- Erkältung
- einen steifen Nacken
- Halsschmerzen

Empfehlung:

- Fußbad
- Kamillentee
- Gymnastik
- vor dem Einschlafen spazierengehen
- zum Zahnarzt gehen
- heißes Wasser mit Whiskey und Zitrone
- Massage
- mit Kamille gurgeln

Was ist das originellste Paar?

5 Medikamente im Internet

Gehen Sie auf *www.accesslanguages.com* und sehen Sie, welche der folgenden Kategorien Sie dort finden können.

- Slimming aids
- Herbal remedies
- Acupuncture
- Vitamins
- Women's health
- Homeopathic remedies

6 In der Apotheke

A Hören Sie dieses Gespräch in der Apotheke, und notieren Sie die Wörter, die Sie hören.

> Kopfschmerzen   Rückenschmerzen   Ohrenschmerzen
> Schlafstörungen   Paracetamol   Aspirin   Lavendelöl
> Schlaftabletten   Vitamine   Migräne

B Hören Sie das Gespräch noch einmal an und beantworten Sie dann die Fragen auf deutsch.

1 • Warum ist Brigitte in der Apotheke?

2 • War sie schon beim Arzt?

3 • Möchte sie Schlaftabletten?

4 • Was empfiehlt der Apotheker?

5 • Was nimmt Brigitte?

6 • Was muß sie bezahlen?

7 • Wieviel Wechselgeld bekommt sie?

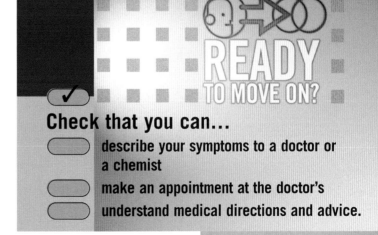

READY TO MOVE ON?

Check that you can...

- describe your symptoms to a doctor or a chemist
- make an appointment at the doctor's
- understand medical directions and advice.

Beim Arzt **UNIT 7**

In Unit 6, you used prepositions which take the accusative case (see page 85). In Exercise 6 on page 107, two more prepositions taking the dative case were introduced: **in** and **bei**. Don't be daunted by these prepositions. As you use them more frequently you will begin to make the necessary changes almost automatically. The most important thing is to remember the gender of the noun.

Prepositions taking the dative case

mit	*with*	nach	*after*	zu	*to*
außer	*except*	seit	*since*	aus	*from (towns, countries), out of (a container)*
bei	*at*	von	*from*	gegenüber	*opposite*

A further group of prepositions can take the accusative or the dative. These **Wechselpräpositionen** (*alternating prepositions*) take either case, depending on their use in the sentence. The main difference is that when a sense of movement is conveyed, the accusative case is used, and for position or location, the dative case is used.

Die Mutter geht in die Küche. ——→ movement ——→ accusative
Die Mutter ist in der Küche. ——→ position ——→ dative

Wechselpräpositionen

an	*by, at*	unter	*under, beneath*	hinter	*behind, after*
in	*in*	neben	*next to*	zwischen	*between*
auf	*on, on top of, onto*	vor	*before, in front of*	über	*over, above*

The dative case leads to certain changes to the endings of articles and prepositions. This table shows the changes from the nominative, i.e. the initial case.

The prepositions **an** and **bei**, used with neuter and masculine nouns, are combined with the articles as follows:

an + dem = am   in + dem = im
bei + dem = beim

The preposition **zu** used with masculine, neuter and feminine nouns is also combined with the articles:

zu + der = zur   zu + dem = zum

	Nominative	Dative
masc.	der	dem
	ein	ein**em**
fem.	die	der
	eine	ein**er**
neut.	das	dem
	ein	ein**em**
plural	die	den

Although there are more changes for the dative than for the accusative case, the changes still follow a specific pattern for definite and indefinite articles.

9 Was ist die Zimmernummer?

 Hören Sie das kurze Gespräch an und beantworten Sie dann die folgende Frage auf deutsch:

Was ist Alisons Zimmernummer im Hotel?

10 Wenn etwas schief geht ...

Luckily, the staff at the hotel where Alison is staying have been very helpful. Sometimes, however, things do not go quite so smoothly.

A Was paßt zu welchem Bild?

a

b

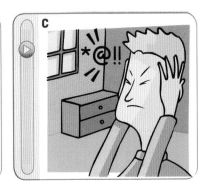

c

d

e

Rezeption

1 • Das Zimmer ist viel zu klein!

2 • Das Essen ist furchtbar!

3 • Das Zimmer hat kein Bad!

4 • Das Zimmer ist zu laut!

5 • Wo ist mein Zimmer? Ich habe eins gebucht!

7 Üben Sie

 Practise the use of prepositions in these phrases. Remember to combine articles and prepositions where necessary.

	Accusative			Dative	
1 •	in	Kirche	in		Kirche
2 •	an	Wand	an		Wand
3 •	gegen	Mauer	bei		Park
4 •	in	Straßen	in		Straßen
5 •	in	Schule	zu		Schule
6 •	in	Theater	in		Theater
7 •	auf	Turm	bei		Post
8 •	in	Kino	in		Kino
9 •	an	Fenster	an		Fenster
10 •	auf	Tisch	auf		Tisch
11 •	auf	Bank	auf		Bank
12 •	in	Park	in		Park
13 •	an	Hotel	an		Hotel

die Post	die Schule	der Tisch
das Kino	die Kirche	das Fenster
das Theater	ein Konzert	ein Café
der Park	die Wand	die Straßen
ein Restaurant	eine Show	das Hotel
die Bank	der Turm	die Mauer

Tell your zur from your zum with more practice on our website.

Beim Arzt UNIT 7

8 Jetzt sind Sie dran!

A (A C) ✎ ▷ Ergänzen Sie die Sätze.

Dative or accusative?

1 • Die Kaffeekanne ist auf ( ) Tisch.

2 • Der neue Film läuft in ( ) Babylon.

3 • Mein Mann bringt die Kinder zu ( ) Schule.

4 • Vor ( ) Fenster haben wir einen wunderschönen Kastanienbaum.

5 • Jedes Zimmer hat ein Barometer an ( ) Wand.

6 • Das habe ich in ( ) Lexikon gelesen!

7 • Mein Vater arbeitet bei ( ) Post.

8 • Wir wohnen in ( ) Park-Hotel.

B ✎ ▷ Beschreiben Sie das Bild.

Beispiel:

Das Buch ist auf dem Tisch.

C ✎ ▷ Wie sagt man das auf deutsch?

1 • You can buy stamps at the post office.

2 • There is a swimming pool behind the house.

3 • Every morning I take the children to school.

4 • We eat in the kitchen.

5 • Goethe's *Faust* is on at the theatre.

6 • You can buy the ticket on the Internet. (im Internet)

7 • We have reserved a room at the Ibis Hotel in Leipzig.

8 • My passport is on the table.

9 • The cat is under the table.

10 • The phone is on the desk.

D 🎲 🎲 ▷ Noch ein Spiel.

Choose six prepositions from the lists in Exercise 7 on page 109 and prepare a die by sticking a preposition in the place of each number.

Beispiel:

1 = an   **2** = zu   **3** = bei

Play with two or three other students. One of you throws the die and the others then have two minutes to write down as many combinations of the preposition plus nouns as possible.

Beim Arzt UNIT

B  Sehen Sie sich die folgenden Cartoons an. Was sagen die Leute?
Benutzen Sie Ihr Glossar oder ein Wörterbuch.

C Beschweren Sie sich! Was ist hier los?

Arbeiten Sie mit einem Partner. Sie sind der Gast, und Ihr Partner ist der
Manager des Hotels auf der nächsten Seite.

(A) **Gast:**
Mein Zimmer ist nass –
das Dach ist nämlich
kaputt.

(B) **Manager:**
Das tut mir leid,
aber die Dachdecker
kommen am Dienstag.

UNIT 7

LEARNING TIP:

In the letter on the following page, you will find a number of verbs used in a form you are not yet familiar with. This is because the author of the letter relates something that happened in the past. Do not be alarmed by a new tense form – it will not impede your understanding of the gist in general. As is often the case in a new language, the context will help you to understand the main ideas of the text.

11 So ein Hotel!

A Lesen Sie den Text an der nächster Seite und entscheiden Sie dann, welche Zusammenfassung korrekt ist: **1** oder **2**?

1 Walter Schmidt was not very happy about his recent stay at the Hotel Marienhof and is asking for compensation due to the serious inadequacies of the hotel.

2 Walter Schmidt is complaining to the manager of the Hotel Marienhof. He is complaining about inadequacies in the hotel and also about the unhelpfulness of staff. He is not asking for compensation, but for a letter of apology from the manager.

Frankfurt, 13. Juni

Sehr geehrter Herr Uhlig,

ich wende mich an Sie, nachdem ich letzte Woche in Ihrem Hotel Marienhof
verbracht habe. Ich reise beruflich viel und habe dadurch in vielen Hotels
in Deutschland und Europa übernachtet. Dabei habe ich verschiedene Standards
kennengelernt und denke, daß ich mir ein Urteil über die Qualität eines Hotels
erlauben kann.

Was ich letzte Woche in Ihrem Hotel erlebt habe, ist mir in meiner ganzen
beruflichen Laufbahn noch nie passiert. Meine drei Tage in Ihrem Hotel waren
ein ganzer Katalog von Fehlern und Katastrophen, und ich möchte Ihnen daher
meine Beschwerden zur Kenntnis bringen.

Mein Leihwagen hatte eine Panne, und ich bin daher relativ spät angekommen.
Ich hatte allerdings per Handy Ihre Rezeption auf dem laufenden gehalten. Die
Kollegin an der Rezeption versicherte mir auch, daß meine Ankunft gegen 21 Uhr
kein Problem sein würde. Als ich dann aber kurz nach 21 Uhr im Hotel ankam,
stellte sich heraus, daß mein Zimmer nicht ein Zimmer mit Badezimmer, wie
bestellt, sondern nur ein Zimmer mit Dusche war. Ich gebe zu, daß das kein
großes Problem war, aber wenn ich ein Zimmer mit Bad bestelle, dann erwarte ich
auch ein Zimmer mit Bad.

Als ich dann ins Restaurant kam, wurde mir gesagt, daß ich kein warmes Essen
mehr bekommen kann, obwohl die Rezeption garantiert hatte, daß das kein Problem
sein würde. Ich muß außerdem sagen, daß der Kellner ausgesprochen unhöflich und
schlecht gelaunt war. Ich hatte das Gefühl, daß ich mich entschuldigen müßte.

Als ich dann hungrig in mein Zimmer ging, fand ich, daß die Klimaanlage im
Zimmer nicht funktionierte und daß das Zimmer viel zu kalt war. Im Schrank war
zwar eine extra Decke, aber auch die war nicht genug.

Ich könnte noch viele solche Katastrophen beschreiben, aber ich denke, daß Sie
jetzt einen Eindruck von meinem Aufenthalt in Ihrem Hotel haben.

Ich erwarte, daß Sie mir mitteilen, was Sie
unternommen haben, um die Mißstände in Ihrem
Hotel abzustellen. Ich denke auch, daß die
Qualität des Hotels während meines Aufenthalts
so schlecht war, daß ich zumindest eine
Teilrückerstattung meiner Rechnung erwarten kann.

Bis zum Empfang Ihres Briefes verbleibe ich
zunächst mit freundlichen Grüßen.

Ihr

Walter Schmidt

Schlüsselwörter

beruflich reisen	*to travel on business*
kennenlernen	*to get to know*
der Leihwagen	*hire care*
unhöflich	*impolite, rude*
die Klimaanlage	*air conditioning*
der Aufenthalt	*stay*

B Lesen Sie die Beschwerden unten. Welche Beschwerden können Sie im Brief lesen?

- The room is too small.
- The hotel is too noisy.
- The food is awful.
- The bathroom was not clean.
- The room was stuffy.
- The waiter was unhelpful.
- The room was double-booked.
- The air conditioning was faulty.

C Ergänzen Sie die Wörter.

1 • Das Zimmer hat kein ( ).

2 • Dic Klimaanlagc ( ) nicht.

3 • Es gab kein warmes ( ) mehr.

4 • Das Zimmer war zu ( ).

12 Jetzt sind Sie dran!

You are staying for two weeks at the Hotel Seeblick in Markdorf at Lake Constance. You are not very happy with the hotel. While on a short trip away during the middle of your stay, you decide to fax the hotel a letter with your complaints, in the hope that they will act on them before you return.

- Das Zimmer ist zu laut.
- Ihr Nachbar spielt die ganze Nacht Musik.
- Das Essen ist immer kalt.

13 Sagen Sie Ihre Meinung!

LANGUAGE FOCUS

In Germany, it is quite acceptable to be forthright about a service you feel does not come up to scratch. The phrases on the right may be helpful.

Agreement

Genau!

Stimmt!

Das finde ich auch!

Ich möchte dem zustimmen!

Da haben Sie Recht!

Das finde ich auch.

Ganz meine Meinung!

Disagreement

Das finde ich nicht.

Aber im Gegenteil!

Das kann doch nicht Ihr Ernst sein!

Lächerlich!

Diskutieren Sie in der Klasse: Ist es gut, immer die Meinung zu sagen? Soll man sich immer beschweren?

ehrlich   die Meinung sagen   Der Kunde ist König!

arrogant   den Service verbessern   diskutieren

Recht haben   hilfreich

zu kritisch   auf die Nerven gehen

Beim Arzt

GLOSSARY 🔊

Nouns

Anwendung (f)	application (here: indication)
Ausflug (m)	excursion
Bauchschmerzen (pl)	stomach ache
Beschwerde (f)	complaint
Dach (n)	roof
Dachdecker (m)	roofer
Erkältung (f)	(a) cold
Fehler (m)	fault, mistake
Formular (n)	form
Geburtstag (m)	birthday
Grippe (f)	flu
Halsschmerzen (pl)	sore throat
Hausbesuch (m)	(doctor's) home visit
Kaffeekanne (f)	coffee pot
Kastanienbaum (m)	horse chestnut tree
Kopfschmerzen (pl)	headache
Laufbahn (f)	career
Leihwagen (m)	hire car
Lexikon (n)	dictionary, encyclopaedia
Migräne (f)	migraine
Mittag (m)	midday, lunchtime
Patient (m)	patient
Rückenschmerzen (pl)	backache
Schlafstörung (f)	insomnia
Schlaftablette (f)	sleeping pill
Tablette (f)	tablet
Tagesdosis (f)	daily dose
Telefongespräch (n)	telephone conversation
Termin (m)	appointment
Trockenpulver (n)	powder
Wand (f)	wall
Wechselgeld (n)	change
Wirkstoff (m)	active ingredient
Wochenende (n)	weekend
Zusammensetzung (f)	composition
Zitrone (f)	lemon
Zahnschmerzen (pl)	toothache
Zimmernummer (f)	room number

Adjectives

furchtbar	awful
nass	wet
unhöflich	impolite

Verbs

bezahlen	to pay
enthalten	to contain
sich wenden an	to approach
übernachten	to spend the night
verordnen	to prescribe

Adverbs

beruflich	on business

Prepositions

an	on, at
auf	on (top), on (to)
aus	from (place)
außer	apart from

GLOSSARY

bei	at	**von**	from (time)
gegenüber	opposite	**zu**	to
hinter	behind	**zwischen**	(in) between
in	in		
mit	with	### Phrases	
nach	after	**auf dem Laufenden halten**	to keep someone updated
neben	next to		
seit	since, for	**… ist schief gegangen**	… went wrong
über	over, across	**schlecht gelaunt sein**	to be in a bad mood
unter	under, underneath		
vor	in front of	**zur Kenntnis bringen**	to bring to the attention of

LOOKING FORWARD

In Unit 8, you will learn more about working in Germany. You will also learn how to express something that happened in the recent past. Here is a website with lots of information related to the topic of work. Who would be searching this website? What information can you expect to find?

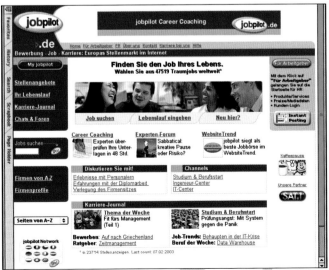

UNIT 7
Was haben Sie nach der Schule gemacht?

Beim Arzt **UNIT 7**

UNIT 8
Was haben Sie nach der Schule gemacht?

We suggest that you come back to this checklist as you progress through the unit. You can then judge how you are getting on.

1 Wissen Sie noch?

A  Dativpräpositionen. Wählen Sie die richtige Präposition.

Rätsel: Ich stehe ( ) einem großen Gebäude. Viele Menschen kommen

( ) dem Taxi oder ( ) dem Bus. Was machen sie hier? Sie

haben viele Koffer und Taschen. ( ) dem Schalter steht eine

Schlange. Eine freundliche Frau gibt Tickets aus. ( ) der Frau läuft ein

Fließband. Darauf stehen die Koffer und Taschen. Die Tickets kommen

( ) dem Drucker ( ) dem Tisch. ( ) einer

großen Anzeigetafel stehen die Abflugs- und Ankunftszeiten.

Wo bin ich? ( ) dem ( )

B Wechselpräpositionen. Wählen Sie die richtige Präposition.
Entscheiden Sie, ob Sie den Dativ oder den Akkusativ brauchen.

Note that none of the prepositions has been combined with the corresponding articles.

1 • Die Ausstellung ist in ( ) Marienkirche.

2 • Im August fahren wir an ( ) Nordsee.

3 • Heute Abend möchte ich nicht kochen. Können wir nicht in ( ) griechische Restaurant am Markt gehen?

4 • Wenn du fertig bist mit der Zeitung, lege sie bitte auf ( ) Tisch.

5 • Wo ist denn mein Regenmantel? – Der ist schon in ( ) Koffer!

6 • Stell doch bitte mal die Blumen auf ( ) Tisch.

7 • Der Wein steht in ( ) Keller.

8 • Hängen Sie doch bitte Ihren Mantel an ( ) Garderobe.

9 • Bei meiner Mutter hängen zu viele Bilder an ( ) Wand.

10 • Wollen wir morgen in ( ) Kino gehen?

Which of the prepositions above would you combine with the articles which follow them?

LEARNING TIP:

Remember that when the preposition describes a position, you need the dative. When, on the other hand, it describes a direction, you need the accusative.

Was haben Sie gemacht?

8

C ✎ ▷ Das Restaurant, wo nichts funktioniert. Welches Adjektiv paßt wo?

> langsam   kalt   klein   alt
> laut   klein   dick   sauer

1 • Der Tisch ist zu (   ).

2 • Die Musik ist zu (   ).

3 • Die Portionen sind zu (   ).

4 • Das Brot ist zu (   ).

5 • Die Soße ist zu (   ).

6 • Die Suppe ist zu (   ).

7 • Der Wein ist zu (   ).

8 • Der Service ist zu (   ).

2 Ein Wiedersehen

A 🎧 ✎ ▷ Hören Sie den Dialog an, und schreiben Sie dann mindestens acht Wörter und drei Zahlen auf, die Sie hören.

B (🎧) ⏺ Hören Sie den Dialog noch einmal und entscheiden Sie dann,
ob die Sätze von 1 bis 10 richtig oder falsch sind.

		Richtig	Falsch
1 •	Barbara and Frank have not seen each other for a couple of years.	⬭	⬭
2 •	Barbara works as a journalist for a national newspaper.	⬭	⬭
3 •	She read German Studies after her A levels.	⬭	⬭
4 •	She then became a teacher of German.	⬭	⬭
5 •	Frank trained as a car mechanic after school.	⬭	⬭
6 •	He stayed in the job for five years.	⬭	⬭
7 •	He now works in the IT industry.	⬭	⬭
8 •	He designs networks and databases.	⬭	⬭
9 •	Barbara is also an IT expert.	⬭	⬭
10 •	Frank is divorced.	⬭	⬭

C (🎧) ✏️ ⏺ Hören Sie den Dialog noch einmal und ergänzen
Sie dann die Sätze.

1 • Frank und Barbara haben sich seit ⬭ Jahren
nicht gesehen.

2 • Frank ist ⬭ geworden.

3 • Barbara hat ⬭ studiert.

4 • Frank hat eine Lehre als ⬭ gemacht.

5 • Frank hat mit ⬭ geheiratet.

6 • Barbara hat mit dem ⬭ gewartet.

7 • Barbara hat ihren Mann vor ⬭ Jahren kennengelernt.

8 • Frank hat nicht ⬭ als Mechaniker gearbeitet.

> Mechaniker
> Germanistik
> zehn   lange
> grau   fünf
> dreiundzwanzig
> Heiraten

Was haben Sie gemacht?

LANGUAGE FOCUS

Perfect tense

The people in Exercise 2C had not seen each other for some time, and when a chance meeting brought them together again, they were busy catching up with each other's news. Because this included lots of things that happened in the past, they used a different tense to express action in the recent past: the perfect tense.

The perfect tense is used to express events in the past and is always used in spoken German. It is also used increasingly in written German.

To form the perfect tense, a new verb form – the past participle – is needed.

Past participles

Past participles also exist in English (e.g. broken, learnt). They are used to form the past tense with either **haben** or **sein**.

haben/sein + past participle → perfect tense
* **Ich habe studiert.** *I (have) studied.*

In the dialogue, did you notice where the participles were positioned in the sentence?

The auxiliary verb (**haben** or **sein**) in the appropriate form is in second position, and the past participle comes last. (See also separable verbs in Unit 3, page 37.) Most verbs use **haben** to form their past participle.

Below are the most important verbs that use **sein** rather than **haben**:

fahren	fallen	fliegen	gehen
geschehen	kommen	laufen	
passieren	reisen	rennen	
schwimmen	sein	springen	
verschwinden	wachsen	werden	

Page 182 shows a complete list of all past participles for verbs used in this course, and as you get used to using this tense form, you will begin to learn the new forms. Don't be daunted by the prospect of a long list of participles to learn. The perfect-tense form presents a step forward in your language-learning process. It will enable you to hold more natural and complex conversations.

Nach der Schule	habe	ich Germanistik	studiert.
Mit 23	habe	ich	geheiratet.
Ich	habe	gestern zwei Filme	gesehen.

D  Hören Sie den Dialog noch einmal und ergänzen Sie drei Verben im Perfekt:

Beispiel:

- geheiratet ● geworden
- ( ) ● ( ) ● ( )

3 Sie sind dran!

Ergänzen Sie die Sätze mit den Partizipien von Übung 2.

1 ● Mein Bruder hat eine Lehre als Tischler ( ).

2 ● Ich habe Anglistik an der Universität in Heidelberg ( ).

3 ● Den neuen Film von Steven Spielberg habe ich schon drei mal ( ).

4 ● Hast du lange auf den Bus ( )?

5 ● Hast du meine Tasche ( )?

6 ● Meine Großmutter hat meinen Großvater mit 18 ( ).

7 ● Nach dem Studium habe ich ein Jahr in Afrika ( ).

8 ● Mein Sohn hat nie Geld. Jetzt hat er den ganzen Sommer ( ).

You'll find more practice on the past tense on our website

4 Was wissen Sie über Barbara und Frank?

A  Arbeiten Sie mit einem Partner. Sagen Sie alles, was Sie über Barbara und Frank wissen. Beginnen Sie mit Barbara.

What facts can you guess?

- Wie lange hat Barbara studiert? ● Wo hat sie studiert?

Barbara hat nach dem Studium … Frank hat nach der Schule …

UNIT **8**

B ✏️ ● Ergänzen Sie *bin* oder *habe*.

Am Samstag feiern wir eine Party. Ich (＿＿＿) schon alles organisiert. Zuerst (＿＿＿) ich eine Liste geschrieben für die Gäste. Dann (＿＿＿) ich das Essen geplant. Dann (＿＿＿) ich in die Stadt gefahren. Dort (＿＿＿) ich alles eingekauft. Letztes Wochenende (＿＿＿) ich dann das Essen gekocht. Weil das Wetter schön wird, (＿＿＿) ich nur leichtes Essen geplant. Für den Empfang der Gäste, (＿＿＿) ich kleine Häppchen gebacken. Ich (＿＿＿) ungefähr vier pro Person gemacht. Als Hauptgericht (＿＿＿) ich Lasagne gemacht. Ich (＿＿＿) vier große Portionen vorbereitet. Die (＿＿＿) ich dann in den Gefrierschrank getan. Jetzt muß ich nur noch ein neues Kleid kaufen, und dann kann die Party kommen!

5 Meine persönliche Geschichte

A 🎲 🎧 ● Lesen Sie die Geschichte von Barbaras Großmutter. Wählen Sie alle Partizipien (es gibt ein Beispiel).

Was willst du denn über mein Leben wissen? Ich habe ein schönes, langes Leben gehabt. Ich bin jetzt fast hundert Jahre alt. Ich bin also Anfang des zwanzigsten Jahrhunderts geboren, 1907, und habe den ersten Weltkrieg als Kind erlebt. Das war furchtbar. Mein Vater ist im Krieg gefallen, ganz am Ende, und meine Mutter war ganz allein mit fünf Kindern. Sie hat so schwer gearbeitet! Sie hat bei den reichen Leuten in den Villen in der Vorstadt saubergemacht. Meine ältere Schwester Lisbeth hat inzwischen auf die kleinen Kinder aufgepaßt. Ich habe ihr viel geholfen, denn ich war die Zweitälteste. Meine Mutter hat nicht viel Geld verdient für die schwere Arbeit. Abends hat sie dann unseren Haushalt noch gemacht und für uns Kinder Kleider genäht oder Pullover gestrickt. Wir Mädchen haben auch viel gestrickt, vor allem Socken! Wir haben alte Pullover wieder aufgetrennt und dann Socken gestrickt. Das ist gar nicht so einfach, du brauchst fünf Nadeln und viel Geduld…

Mit zwanzig habe ich dann deinen Großvater kennengelernt. Er hat auf dem Land gearbeitet, bei einem Junker in der Mark Brandenburg. Vierzehn Stunden am Tag, sechs Tage die Woche. Aber am Sonntag haben wir dann etwas zusammen gemacht: wir sind viel mit dem Fahrrad gefahren und spazierengegangen. Ein Jahr später, haben wir dann geheiratet und ich bin zu ihm auf's Land gezogen. Und dann zwei Jahre später habe ich deine Tante Karin bekommen und dann 1935 deine Mutter. Wir haben in einer kleinen Kate auf dem Gut gewohnt, und ich habe Arbeit im Gutshaus bekommen.

Dann kam der Zweite Weltkrieg, und dein Großvater mußte Soldat werden. Schon nach vier Monaten wurde er verwundet und kam wieder nach Hause. Ich habe ihn dann gesundgepflegt, und weil er einen Arm verloren hatte, konnte er auch zu Hause bleiben. Nach dem Krieg sind wir dann nach Berlin gezogen, das war gleich 1945, im Juli, glaube ich. Den Rest kennst du ja … Vielleicht sollte ich einmal unsere Familiengeschichte aufschreiben. Ich habe auch irgendwo einen Stammbaum.

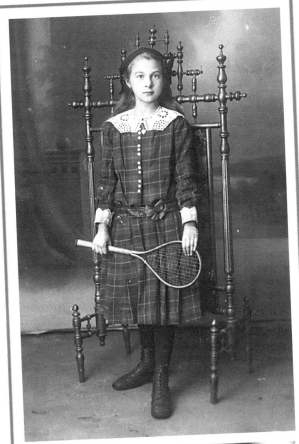

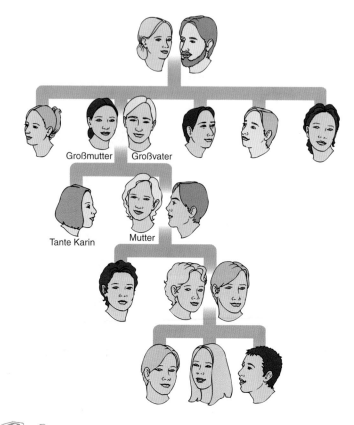

Großmutter Großvater

Tante Karin Mutter

B 🅰🅲 ✏️ 💿 Lesen Sie den Text noch einmal, und beantworten Sie dann die folgenden Fragen.

1 • How old is Barbara's grandmother?

2 • What did you find out about her parents?

3 • How many siblings did she have?

4 • What did her eldest sister have to do?

5 • When did she meet her future husband?

6 • How many children did she have?

7 • What happened to her husband in World War II?

8 • Where did they move to after the war?

C A C ✏ 🕐 Lesen Sie den Text noch einmal, und ergänzen Sie dann die Informationen.

1907   Barbaras Großmutter ist (   ) worden.

1918   Ihr Vater ist (   ) (   ) (   ).

(   )   Barbaras Großmutter hat ihren zukünftigen Mann kennengelernt.

(   )   Die Großmutter hat geheiratet.

(   )   Die Großmutter hat ihr erstes Kind bekommen.

(   )   Die Großmutter hat ihr zweites Kind bekommen.

1945   Die Großmutter ist nach Berlin (   ).

D 🗣 👥 🕐 Arbeiten Sie mit einem Partner. Ein Partner stellt Fragen zum Lebenslauf von Barbaras Großmutter, der andere Partner antwortet.

Frage: Wann ist Barbaras Großmutter geboren worden?

Antwort: (   )

6 Hören Sie mal

🎧 ✏ 🕐 Hören Sie die Biografien von einigen berühmten Menschen aus dem deutschsprachigen Raum, und ergänzen Sie dann die fehlenden Jahreszahlen.

1 • Ludwig van Beethoven wurde (   ) geboren.

2 • Schon (   ) hat er in einem Orchester gespielt.

3 • (   ) ist er nach Wien gezogen.

4 • Seine neunte Sinfonie hat er (   ) geschrieben.

Was haben Sie gemacht? UNIT **8**

5 • Georg Friedrich Händel wurde ⌐⎯⎯⎯⎯⎯⎯⎯⏋ in Halle an der Saale geboren.

6 • Von ⌐⎯⎯⎯⎯⎯⏋ bis ⌐⎯⎯⎯⎯⎯⏋ hat er eine Reise nach Italien gemacht.

7 • ⌐⎯⎯⎯⎯⎯⏋ hat er als Hofkapellmeister in Hamburg gearbeitet.

8 • ⌐⎯⎯⎯⎯⎯⏋ ist er nach London gezogen.

9 • Siegmund Freud wurde ⌐⎯⎯⎯⎯⎯⏋ in Österreich geboren.

10 • Von ⌐⎯⎯⎯⎯⎯⏋ an hat er einige Jahre an der Universität in Wien gearbeitet.

11 • ⌐⎯⎯⎯⎯⎯⏋ ist er nach London emigriert.

12 • Clara Schumann wurde ⌐⎯⎯⎯⎯⎯⏋ in Leipzig geboren.

13 • ⌐⎯⎯⎯⎯⎯⏋ hat sie Robert Schumann geheiratet.

14 • Von ⌐⎯⎯⎯⎯⎯⏋ bis ⌐⎯⎯⎯⎯⎯⏋ hat sie als Lehrerin am Konservatorium in Frankfurt gearbeitet.

7 Sie sind dran!

A Arbeiten Sie mit einem Partner. Fragen Sie Ihren Partner einige neugierige Fragen, wie unten. Wenn Ihr Partner geantwortet hat, ist er dran mit den Fragen.

Don't forget you do not have to answer every question truthfully. Assume a different biography if you prefer!

- Wann sind Sie geboren worden?
- Wo sind Sie geboren worden?
- Wann sind Sie zur Schule gegangen?
- Wann haben Sie in Ihrem ersten Job gearbeitet?
- Wo haben Sie zuerst gearbeitet?

B Erzählen Sie jetzt der Gruppe, was Sie erfahren haben.

> ... ist ... geboren worden.
> ... ist ... zur Schule gekommen.
> ... hat ...

8 Was ist passiert?

A Hören Sie das Gespräch in der Hotelrezeption. Entscheiden Sie dann, ob der Cartoon in **a** oder der Cartoon in **b** die Situation korrekt beschreibt.

a

b

B  Hören Sie das Gespräch noch einmal. Beantworten Sie dann die Fragen unten auf Deutsch.

1 • Warum hat er das Zimmer 112 nicht genommen?

2 • Welches Zimmer hat er im Hotel bekommen?

3 • Wohin ist der Gast in den Urlaub gefahren?

4 • Was ist mit den Koffern passiert?

5 • Was haben sie auf dem Flughafen gekauft?

READY TO MOVE ON?

Check that you can...

- understand how the perfect tense is formed
- understand biographical data from listening or reading
- express some basic biographical data for yourself.

9 Noch eine Biographie

Was hat Stefanie wann gemacht?

1962	Abteilungsleiterin geworden
1968	nach der Lehre in eine Stelle übernommen
1974	geboren
1978	in die Sekundarschule gekommen
1981	auf das Gymnasium gegangen
1981–1983	in die Primarschule gekommen
1983–1994	bei der Post mehrere Stellen gehabt
1994	Abitur gemacht
1983	eine Lehre bei der Post gemacht

10 Wie schreibt man eine perfekte Bewerbung?

Although job applications through the Internet are becoming increasingly popular, there are still a large number of more conventional applications written in the time-honoured manner of a letter and a CV.

A Lesen Sie, was die jungen Leute schreiben, die sich um eine Ausbildung oder Lehre bewerben.

Wissen Sie, wie man sich bewirbt?

Nancy

Ich habe mich erfolgreich um eine Ausbildungsstelle beworben. Geholfen hat mir sicherlich, daß ich mich ausführlich über den entsprechenden Beruf informiert hatte und deutlich machen konnte, daß meine Interessen dazu passen.

Martin

Ich kann mir ungefähr vorstellen, wie ein Bewerbungsschreiben auszusehen hat. Sobald bei mir allerdings der Bewerbungsstreß so richtig losgeht, werde ich mich eingehender informieren – beim Arbeitsamt oder mittels Literatur.

Anselm

Man bewirbt sich mit einem tabellarischen Lebenslauf. Dieser muß natürlich sauber, leserlich und fehlerfrei geschrieben sein. Dazu legt man sein Zeugnis und falls nötig noch ein Paßbild.

Jasmin

Ich habe mir von Freunden Bücher über die richtige Bewerbung ausgeliehen und mich so kundig gemacht. Ich glaube, es ist sehr wichtig, über dieses Thema Bescheid zu wissen, da man nur mit einer guten Bewerbung Aussicht auf Erfolg hat.

Ulrike

Ich habe bereits 22 Bewerbungen geschrieben und nun endlich einen Ausbildungsplatz gefunden. Infos zum Thema Bewerbung bekam ich von Freunden und Bekannten. Hilfreiche Tipps fand ich auch in Büchern.

Was kann man tun, damit die Bewerbung erfolgreich wird? Schreiben Sie fünf Tipps auf.

B Lesen Sie jetzt die Texte noch einmal und beantworten Sie dann die folgenden Fragen auf deutsch.

1 • Wer hat eine Ausbildungsstelle bekommen?

2 • Weiß Martin, wie man einen Bewerbungsbrief schreibt?

3 • Was hat Jasmin für die Bewerbung ausgeliehen?

4 • Welche drei Dinge empfiehlt Anselm für die Bewerbung?

5 • Wieviele Bewerbungen hat Ulrike geschrieben?

6 • Was hat Jasmin vor der Bewerbung gemacht?

7 • Was, denkt Nancy, ist besonders wichtig, damit eine Bewerbung Erfolg hat?

8 • Wie muß der Lebenslauf für eine Bewerbung aussehen?

Practise the comparative on our website.

LANGUAGE FOCUS

Adjectives

Adjectives are words that describe a noun:
Der Wein ist **kalt**.
When comparing two or more nouns, the adjectives are compared, too.

- Robert ist groß. Michael ist größer.
  Serdar ist am größten.
- Wein A ist kalt. Wein B ist kälter.
  Wein C ist am kältesten.

These forms are called the comparative (equivalent of –er/more…) and the superlative (equivalent of –est/most…).

adjective	comparative	superlative
schön	schöner	am schönsten
reich	reicher	am reichsten
klein	kleiner	am kleinsten
rund	runder	am rundesten
lieb	lieber	am liebsten

Adjectives of one syllable with an **a, o** or **u** take an umlaut:

warm	wärmer	am wärmsten
dumm	dümmer	am dümmsten
kalt	kälter	am kältesten
alt	älter	am ältesten
groß	größer	am größten

Some adjectives are irregular, just as in English (e.g. good – better – best):

gut	besser	am besten
nah	näher	am nächsten
viel	mehr	am meisten

When comparing two nouns directly, **als** is used.

- Michael ist größer als Robert.
- Das Buch ist dicker als die Zeitung.
- In München ist es kälter als in Berlin.

11 Jetzt sind Sie dran!

A  Ergänzen Sie die richtige Adjektivform.

1 • Die Hauptstraße ist ( ) als die Nebenstraße. (breit)

2 • Die Elbe ist ( ) als die Elster. (lang)

3 • Die Fahrt auf der Autobahn ist ( ). (schnell)

4 • Meine Schwester ist ( ) als ich. (jung)

5 • Der Regionalzug ist ( ). (langsam)

6 • Indisches Essen ist ( ) als englisches. (scharf)

7 • In Italien ist das Wetter ( ). (gut)

8 • Im Schwimmbad ist das Wasser ( ) als im Meer. (warm)

B Welcher Komparativ paßt? A personnel officer looking through a great number of applications always has something to criticise! Fill in the comparative.

1 • Diese Bewerbung ist zu kurz. Sie könnte etwas ( ) sein.

2 • Dieser Lebenslauf ist nicht sehr ordentlich. Er könnte ( ) sein.

3 • Diese Kandidatin ist nicht gut vorbereitet. Sie könnte ( ) sein.

4 • Diese Bewerbung ist nicht vollständig. Sie könnte ( ) sein.

5 • Der Lebenslauf ist nicht sehr sauber. Er könnte ( ) sein.

6 • Das Photo ist nicht sehr scharf. Es könnte ( ) sein.

7 • Das Begleitschreiben ist zu unklar. Es könnte ( ) sein.

Was haben Sie gemacht? UNIT **8**

12 Testen Sie Ihr Allgemeinwissen!

Teilen Sie die Klasse in zwei Gruppen. Beide Teams müssen dann die Fragen beantworten. Wer gewinnt?

Die Antworten finden Sie auf Seite 137, aber nicht schummeln!

1 • Welches Auto fährt der deutsche Rennfahrer Michael Schumacher?

2 • Wann ist die Berliner Mauer gefallen?

3 • Wer hat *Faust* und *Egmont* geschrieben?

4 • Wer hat den Text für die *Ode an die Freude* geschrieben?

5 • Welche Stadt war die Hauptstadt von Deutschland bis August 1990?

6 • Seit wann gibt es den Euro in Deutschland?

7 • Wie heißt der erfolgreichste deutsche Tennisspieler?

8 • Wie heißt die erfolgreichste deutsche Tennisspielerin?

9 • Wer war der letzte deutsche Kaiser?

10 • Welcher deutsche Bundeskanzler hat die Wiedervereinigung erlebt?

11 • Wo ist das Brandenburger Tor?

12 • Was hat in 1945 in Potsdam stattgefunden?

GLOSSARY

Nouns

Abteilungsleiter (m)	head of department
Anfang (m)	beginning
Anglistik (f)	English studies
Ankunft (f)	arrival
Ausstellung (f)	exhibition
Bild (n)	picture
Bewerbung (f)	application
Drucker (m)	printer
Fahrt (f)	journey
Flughafen (m)	airport
Gebäude (n)	building
Gefrierschrank (m)	freezer
Geld (n)	money

GLOSSARY

Germanistik (f)	German Studies	**griechisch**	Greek
Gut (n)	large farm-holding	**kalt**	cold
Gutshaus (n)	family home belonging to the gentry	**reich**	rich
		sauer	sour
		zukünftig	future

Germanistik (f) — German Studies
Gut (n) — large farm-holding
Gutshaus (n) — family home belonging to the gentry

Jahrhundert (n) — century
Junker (m) — landed aristocrat
Kate (f) — small farm worker's cottage
Kleid (n) — dress
Koffer (m) — suitcase
Leben (n) — life
Lebenslauf (m) — CV, biography
Lehre (f) — apprenticeship
Mechaniker (m) — mechanic
Regenmantel (m) — raincoat
Regionalzug (m) — regional train
Schalter (m) — counter
Schlange (f) — queue (also *snake*)
Stammbaum (m) — family tree
Stelle (f) — job, position
Studium (n) — university course
Tasche (f) — case, handbag
Tischler (m) — carpenter

Adjectives

deutschsprachig — German-speaking
dick — thick, big
fehlend — missing

griechisch — Greek
kalt — cold
reich — rich
sauer — sour
zukünftig — future

Verbs

aufmachen — to open
fallen — to fall, to die (in action)
geschehen — to happen
heiraten — to get married
nähen — to sew
organisieren — to organise
passieren — to happen
planen — to plan
rennen — to run
saubermachen — to clean
springen — to jump
stricken — to knit
verschwinden — to disappear
wachsen — to grow
werden — to become

Adverbs

zuerst — firstly

Phrases

Erfolg haben — to be successful

Answers to Exercise 12

1 Ferrari   2 1989   3 Goethe   4 Schiller   5 Bonn   6 2002
7 Boris Becker   8 Steffi Graf   9 Wilhelm II.   10 Helmut Kohl
11 Berlin   12 Potsdamer Konferenz

Was haben Sie gemacht? UNIT 8

LOOKING FORWARD

In Unit 9, we will learn more about the world of work and the 'work-life' balance. Look at the two websites below and what they offer and find three ways in which they differ.

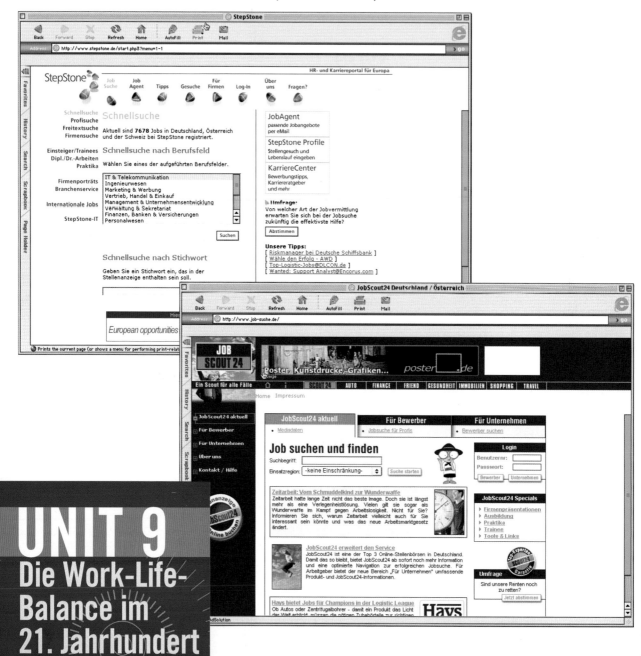

UNIT 9
Die Work-Life-Balance im 21. Jahrhundert

UNIT 9
Die Work-Life-Balance im 21. Jahrhundert

By the end of this unit you will be able to:

- Talk about the concept of work-life balance
- Understand and interpret simple statistics
- Express your opinion and comment on other opinions
- Express predictions
- Express options and preferences (hypothetically and conditionally)
- Use connectors to join different sentences

We suggest that you come back to this checklist as you progress through the unit. You can then judge how you are getting on.

1 Wissen Sie noch?

A 🎲 ✏️ ⏵ Ergänzen Sie den Infinitiv! Remember that sometimes the past participle looks quite different from the infinitive:

Beispiel:

aufgemacht	**aufmachen**	abgeholt	
gehört		gelesen	
angefangen		gedauert	
gelaufen		geschwommen	
eingekauft		gerannt	
gegessen			

B 🎲 ✏️ ⏵ Lesen Sie diese kleine Geschichte, und schreiben Sie die Geschichte auf, als ob sie gestern passiert wäre.

Don't forget to use the perfect tense.

> Ich stehe um sieben Uhr auf. Dann dusche ich und ziehe mich an. Um 7.30 frühstücke ich. Ich esse zwei Scheiben Toast mit Erdbeermarmelade und trinke drei Tassen Kaffee. Zum Zeitunglesen bleibt keine Zeit! Um acht Uhr laufe ich zur Bushaltestelle und fahre mit dem Bus zur Arbeit. Das dauert ungefähr eine halbe Stunde. Von der Bushaltestelle bis zum Büro laufe ich noch einmal ungefähr zehn Minuten. Viertel vor neun komme ich an. Um 13 Uhr gehe ich mit meiner Kollegin in die Kantine. Wir machen eine Mittagspause von 30 Minuten. Ich esse einen Salat und trinke einen Orangensaft, meine Kollegin ißt eine Gemüsesuppe und trinkt auch einen Orangensaft. Um 15 Uhr gehe ich schnell zur Reinigung und hole meinen blauen Hosenanzug ab. Zehn nach fünf mache ich Feierabend und gehe nach Hause. Heute Abend gehe ich mit meiner Schwester ins Kino.

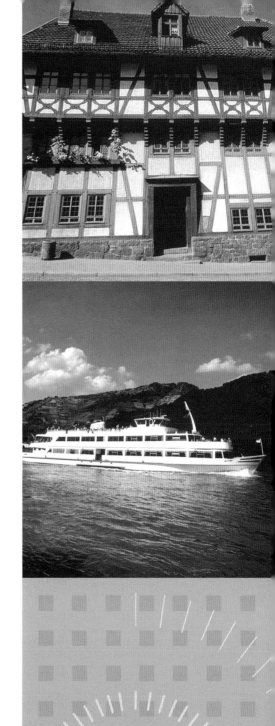

C  Welches Adjektiv paßt?

Fill in the adjective in the correct form. Don't forget to use the comparative form for comparisons. One adjective is used twice.

> **kalt   schwer   voll   leise**
>
> **laut   kompliziert   viel**

1 • Eisen ist (_____) als Sand.

2 • Dein Glas ist (_____) als meins!

3 • Das Radio ist zu (_____). Mach es

(_____)!

4 • Der letzte Computerkurs war am (_____).

5 • In meinem neuen Job verdiene ich (_____)

als in meinem alten.

6 • Unsere Ferienwohnung war viel (_____) als eure.

7 • Die Ostsee ist (_____) als das Schwarze Meer.

8 • Deutsch ist nicht so (_____) wie Englisch!

2 Karriere oder Freizeit?

A 🗣️)) ▶ Sehen Sie sich die Illustration zu dem folgenden Artikel an. Was sind Ihre Prioritäten? Was ist Ihnen am wichtigsten?

Mir ist … am wichtigsten.

Die Bausteine des Lebens
Work-Life-Balance

Karriere oder Freizeit? Das ist heute nicht mehr die Frage. Führungskräfte wollen beides. Die Folge: Sie hetzen von einem Termin zum nächsten und sind irgendwann völlig ausgepowert. Wie aber läßt sich eine gesunde Work-Life-Balance finden? managerSeminare stellt wirkungsvolle Ansätze und Methoden vor.

Fehlen in der Illustration noch andere Prioritäten?

B 🗣️)) 👥 ▶ Arbeiten Sie jetzt mit der ganzen Klasse.
Der Text in dieser Übung heißt 'Karriere oder Freizeit?'
Was denken Sie, worum es in diesem Text geht? Sammeln Sie Ideen!

Es geht um …

LEARNING TIP:
Remember the preposition **um**? You will need to change the articles for masculine nouns into the accusative.

C [A C] ✎ 🎧 ◉ Lesen Sie jetzt den Text, und wählen Sie dann die richtige Antwort für jede Frage. Bevor Sie den Text lesen, sehen Sie sich die Schlüsselwörter an.

Gregor Maier hat wieder einmal schlecht geschlafen. Die schlechten Umsätze des Unternehmens, der ständige Ärger mit seinem unorganisierten Assistenten und die Hetzjagd von einem Meeting zum nächsten machen ihm zu schaffen. Hinzu kommt die Sorge, den hohen Anforderungen im Job nicht gewachsen zu sein: Erst vergangene Woche hat ihn sein Chef kritisiert, daß er das neue Projekt nicht im Griff habe. Dabei hat er doch Tag und Nacht daran gearbeitet. Und dann noch der Streit mit seiner Frau: Mehrmals hat er ihr einen Kinoabend versprochen und dann wegen all dem beruflichen Stress wieder abgesagt – was er sehr bedauert. „Was ist nur los mit mir?", fragt sich Maier nun ständig, findet aber keine Antwort.

Gregor Maier ist kein Einzelfall. Viele Führungskräfte und Selbstständige zwischen 30 und 40 sind unzufrieden mit ihrem Leben. Der Grund: Sie haben ihre Work-Life-Balance, also das ausgewogene Gleichgewicht zwischen Beruf und Privatleben, verloren bzw. noch gar nicht gefunden. Viele fühlen sich zwischen den steigenden Anforderungen im Job und privaten Verpflichtungen und Vergnügungen hin- und hergerissen. Sie wollen sowohl dem Beruf als auch dem Privatleben gerecht werden, wissen aber nicht, wie.

These key words will help you get the gist of the text.

Schlüsselwörter

die Umsätze (pl)	*turnover*
der ständige Ärger	*permanent problems*
die Hetzjagd	*chase*
die Sorge	*worry*
den hohen Anforderungen (nicht) gewachsen sein	*to be up (or not) to the demands of the job*
im Griff haben	*to be on top of something*
der Streit	*row*
absagen	*to cancel*
die Führungskräfte	*senior managers*
Selbstständige	*self-employed (people)*
die Verpflichtungen	*duties*
die Vergnügungen	*enjoyments (also: entertainments)*

1 • Why is Gregor Maier having problems sleeping?
  a He has lost a contract for his boss.
  b He is worried about an order that has not come in yet.
  c He is stressed about a number of problems at work, including his disorganised assistant.

2 • When did his boss criticise his work on the new project?
  a Last week.
  b Last night.
  c Constantly.

3 • Why did he row with his wife?
  a He is always late home from work.
  b He had to cancel the visit to the cinema.
  c He was late arriving at the cinema.

4 • Why are many managers and self-employed people unhappy?
  a They do not feel they get paid enough.
  b They feel they want to do a good job and have a happy private life.
  c They worry about losing their jobs in an increasingly unstable labour market.

D (A C) ✏ ○ Lesen Sie jetzt den Text noch einmal, und ergänzen Sie die Partizipien in den Sätzen.

1 ● Gregor Maier hat wieder einmal schlecht ( ).

2 ● Vergangene Woche hat ihn sein Chef ( ).

3 ● Aber er hat Tag und Nacht an dem Projekt ( ).

4 ● Gregor hat seiner Frau schon mehrmals einen Abend im Kino ( ).

5 ● Aber immer wieder hat er dann ( ).

6 ● Viele Manager haben die 'Work-Life-Balance' ( ) oder noch nicht ( ).

E 🖼 ○ Sehen Sie sich jetzt noch einmal die Illustration an. Stimmen Ihre Prioritäten? Möchten Sie neue Prioritäten ergänzen?

F ✏ ○ Können Sie Gregor Maier helfen?

LEARNING TIP:

Remember, when giving advice you need to use *should* (sollte).

Beispiel:

Ich denke, er sollte mit seinem Assistenten sprechen. Er sollte seinem Assistenten helfen …

The activities on the previous page feature a real-life situation; sometimes one would like to juxtapose this with an 'ideal-life' situation, using the expression *I'd rather…* In German this is quite straightforward:

- Ich würde gern/lieber …
- Ich hätte gern/lieber …

- Ich **arbeite** sechs Tage in der Woche, aber ich **würde lieber** nur vier Tage **arbeiten**.
- Ich **arbeite** in Hamburg, aber ich **würde lieber** in Berlin **arbeiten**.
- Mein Mann **fährt** zweimal in der Woche nach Siegen, aber er **würde lieber** nur einmal in der Woche **fahren**.
- Wir **fahren** im August nach Bayern, aber ich **würde lieber** nach Griechenland **fahren**.

The two parts of the sentences above are linked with **aber** (but). In the second part, **würde** expresses the hypothetical nature of the statement. The main part of the verb, here **arbeiten** and **fahren**, then goes to the end of the sentence.

ich würde	wir würden
du würdest	ihr würdet
er/sie/es würde	sie würden

If you want to say you'd rather have one thing than another, **haben** is used as follows:

- Ich **habe** zwei Kinder, aber ich **hätte** gern sieben!

ich hätte	wir hätten
du hättest	ihr hättet
er/sie/es hätte	sie hätten

Try www.accesslanguages for further practice.

3 Sie sind dran!

  Ergänzen Sie die Sätze.

Make sure to choose the correct second half to complete the sentence. Mind the word order and the correct form of würden or haben.

… nicht am Wochenende …	… weniger essen …
… einen Garten …	… mit dem Fahrrad …
… blonde Locken …	… laufen …
… weniger …	… in einem Einzelhaus …

1 • Ich wohne in einem Reihenhaus,

2 • Mein Mann arbeitet am Wochenende,

3 • Wir haben einen Balkon,

4 • Ich fahre mit dem Zug zur Arbeit,

5 • Meine Tochter hat schwarze Haare,

6 • Leider esse ich sehr gern,

7 • Wir fahren zu oft mit dem Auto,

8 • Sie hat zu viel zu tun,

4 Hören Sie mal!

A Hören Sie mal die Interviews, die ein Reporter für die Radiosendung 'Karriere und Beruf' macht.

Was sagen die Leute?
Wie würden Sie gern arbeiten?

B Hören Sie wieder die Interviews. Ergänzen Sie dann die Informationen in der Tabelle.

1

3

2

4

		Beruf	Alter	Angestellt/Selbständig	Wo?	Wie lange?
1	Friederike		37			30 bis 80 Stunden
2	Holger			angestellt	Schule	
3	Sebastian	Instrumentenbauer				
4	Elke					

C Arbeiten Sie mit einem Partner.
Ein Partner stellt die Fragen, der andere antwortet.

Beispiel:

(A) Frage: Was ist Friederikes Job?

(B) Antwort: Sie ist Trainerin von Beruf.

LANGUAGE FOCUS

Ich finde/Ich glaube

Throughout this book, you have been introduced to a variety of ways of expressing agreement or disagreement. To express assumption and hypothesis, you can use the terms **ich finde …** or **ich glaube …**:

- Ich glaube, Franziska ist Lehrerin von Beruf.

To link the two parts of the sentence more closely, use **daß** (that):

- Ich glaube, **daß** Franziska Lehrerin ist.

Note that the use of **daß** makes the verb move to the end of the sentence.

- Ich glaube, **daß** er in Berlin **wohnt**.
- Meine Mutter sagt immer, **daß** ich zu viel **esse**.

In the perfect tense, the form of **haben** or **sein** goes right to the end of the sentence, following the past participle:

- Bernard hat gesagt, **daß** er das Buch schon **gelesen hat**.
- Ich glaube, **daß** ich das schon **gehört habe**.

D ◉ Diskutieren Sie die Informationen in der Gruppe. Sammeln Sie Argumente. Im Kasten finden Sie einige Vokabeln für die Diskussion.

For a group discussion about work/jobs, try to incorporate your colleagues' reactions into your contribution:

- … hat gesagt, daß…
- Aber ich finde, daß …

Ich finde	Das stimmt (nicht)
Ich glaube	… ist realistisch/unrealistisch
Ich glaube, daß…	Heutzutage arbeiten viele Leute …
	Auf dem heutigen Arbeitsmarkt …
	… würde lieber …
	… sollte …
	… lieber … würde.

E  Wie sieht Ihr Traumjob aus?

Write down a few ideas about your dream job to enable you to report back to the class.

- Ich würde gern als … arbeiten.
- Dann könnte ich …
- Jeden Tag/Jede Woche würde ich …

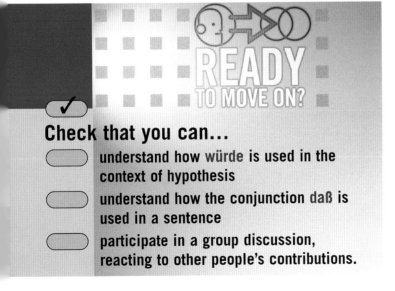

READY TO MOVE ON?

✓

Check that you can…

- understand how **würde** is used in the context of hypothesis
- understand how the conjunction **daß** is used in a sentence
- participate in a group discussion, reacting to other people's contributions.

5 Stress und Ärger im Beruf?

A [AC] ▷ Lesen Sie die folgende Statistik. Erkennen Sie die Symptome?

Die Reaktion von Männern und Frauen auf Stress und Ärger im Beruf.

Männer

nichts sagen:	73%
Sport machen:	65%
in die Kneipe gehen:	58%
mit Freunden reden:	56%
wütend werden:	56%
spazierengehen:	32%
meditieren:	11%

Frauen

nichts sagen:	81%
mit Freunden reden:	78%
Sport machen:	60%
spazierengehen:	57%
wütend werden:	46%
meditieren:	43%
in die Kneipe gehen:	27%

B ▷ Machen Sie jetzt einen Text aus der Statistik.

Beispiel:

Jetzt sagen 73% der Männer nichts, und 81% der Frauen sagen nichts.

LANGUAGE FOCUS

The task of interpreting statistical data can be made more authentic by using words to compare or contrast the two different parts of a sentence, i.e. 73% of men do not say anything, but (by contrast) 81% of women do not say anything.

In German as in English, this contrast is expressed by inserting the word **aber** at the beginning of the second part of the sentence.

- 73% der Männer sagen nichts, aber 81% der Frauen sagen nichts.

When using **aber**, the word order of the second part of the sentence **does not change**. Note that in spoken German, **aber** is not always placed strictly at the beginning of the second part of a sentence.

Because of the function of joining up two parts of the sentence, words like **aber** are called conjunctions. One conjunction that you have been using frequently, without even knowing it, is **und**.

C 🔊 💭 Was machen Sie bei Stress im Beruf?

Manchmal … ich, aber oft … ich.

6 Üben Sie!

Ⓐ ✎ 💭 Was paßt zusammen?

1 • Ich arbeite drei Tage pro Woche im Büro,

2 • Früher hat Mario keinen Alkohol getrunken,

3 • Mein Mann spielt Klavier und Trompete,

4 • Die meisten Leute haben ein Handy,

5 • Nancy feiert heute eine Sommerparty,

6 • Ich würde gern nach Australien fahren,

7 • Meine Tochter möchte gern bis Mitternacht in die Disko gehen,

8 • Peter hat über 30 Jahre bei der Post gearbeitet,

a • aber ich kann leider kein Instrument spielen.

b • aber ich fliege nicht gern.

c • aber jetzt ist er pensioniert.

d • aber wir können nicht gehen.

e • aber sie muß spätestens um 23 Uhr zu Hause sein.

f • aber von Freitag bis Montag bin ich zu Hause.

g • aber heute trinkt er gern Wein zum Essen.

h • aber ich habe immer noch keins.

ACCESS GERMAN

7 Testen Sie sich!

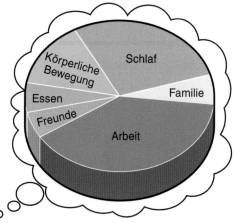

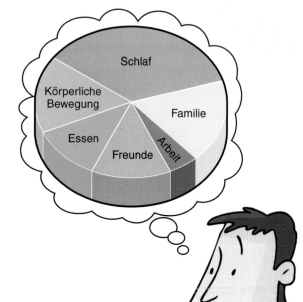

 Wir haben viel über die Balance zwischen Beruf und Privatleben gesprochen. Jetzt machen Sie doch einmal einen Selbsttest. Arbeiten Sie mit einem Partner.

Draw a circle and mark off segments according to how much time, in your opinion, you allocate to the different parts of your life:

- Arbeit
- Schlaf
- Familie/Freunde
- Essen
- körperliche Bewegung/Sport

Sind Sie mit Ihrem Kreis zufrieden? Wenn nicht, machen Sie einen neuen, 'idealen' Kreis.

Fragen Sie sich selbst und Ihren Partner:

- Wie kann ich meine Situation verbessern?
- Habe ich genug Zeit für Dinge eingeplant, die mir wichtig sind?
- Habe ich jeden Tag mindestens eine Mußestunde?
- Erhole ich mich nach jeder Stressperiode?

8 Zwei Freundinnnen unter sich

A  Hören Sie das Gespräch zwischen Martina und Elisabeth. Dann kreuzen Sie an, wer was gesagt hat.

	Martina	Elisabeth
1 • Ich habe zwei Jahre in England gelebt.	◯	◯
2 • Ich bin seit einem Monat wieder da.	◯	◯
3 • Der Trainer hat uns viele Tipps gegeben.	◯	◯
4 • Ich bin oft ganz kaputt.	◯	◯
5 • Ich arbeite wieder Vollzeit.	◯	◯
6 • Ich hatte oft Heimweh.	◯	◯
7 • Ich wollte oft wieder nach Hause kommen.	◯	◯
8 • Ich habc cincn Kursus zum Thema 'time management' besucht.	◯	◯

B 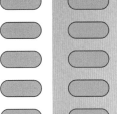 Hören Sie das Gespräch noch einmal. Diskutieren Sie dann in der Klasse die Vorteile und die Nachteile vom Leben im Ausland. Machen Sie Notizen an der Tafel oder auf einem Flipchart.

Vorteile	**Nachteile**

Die Work-Life-Balance im 21. Jahrhundert

C 🔊 👥 ▶ Arbeiten Sie mit einem Partner.
Diskutieren Sie: Würden Sie gern im Ausland leben?

- Ich würde gern im Ausland leben, aber …
- Machmal würde ich gern …

LANGUAGE FOCUS

Previously in this unit, you learnt how to join sentences using **und**
and **aber**. In addition to these conjunctions, however, there are
words known as 'subjunctions' which join different parts of the
sentence but indicate that one of the parts is the main part,
and the other is subordinate. Always remember that
with a subjunction, such as **weil** (*because*), the verb in the second
(subordinate) clause goes to the end:

- Ich würde gern im Ausland leben, weil   das Wetter besser **ist**.
  das Essen besser **ist**.
  ich lieber in der Sonne **lebe**.

9 Üben Sie!

 Was paßt hier am besten: **weil**, **und** oder **aber**?
Ergänzen Sie das richtige Wort.

1 • Mein Bruder ist 20 Jahre alt, ⟨_____⟩ er studiert in Leipzig.

2 • Ich würde gern nochmal studieren, ⟨_____⟩ jetzt habe ich keine Zeit mehr.

3 • Ich bin wieder nach Hause gekommen, ⟨_____⟩ ich eine neue Stelle angefangen habe.

4 • Sophia arbeitet als Sekretärin, ⟨_____⟩ sie möchte lieber als Lehrerin arbeiten.

5 • Ich habe die Wäsche im Haus aufgehängt, ⟨_____⟩ es regnet.

6 • Wir fahren im August nach Dresden ⟨_____⟩ bleiben dort eine Woche.

7 • Er hat das ganze Wochenende gearbeitet, ⟨_____⟩ er einen Bericht schreiben mußte.

8 • Unsere Firma hat ihre großen Büros in Frankfurt und Leipzig, ⟨_____⟩ mein Büro ist in Dömitz.

GLOSSARY

Nouns

Arbeitsmarkt (m)	job market
Argument (n)	argument
Balkon (m)	balcony
Bushaltestelle (f)	bus stop
Einzelhaus (n)	detached house
Eisen (n)	iron
Erdbeermarmelade (f)	strawberry jam
Feierabend (m)	the time after work (literally: the party evening)
Freizeit (f)	spare time
Führungskraft (f)	senior manager
Handy (n)	mobile phone
Heimweh (n)	homesickness
Hetzjagd (f)	chase
Hosenanzug (m)	trouser suit

GLOSSARY

Kantine (f)	canteen
Kasten (m)	box
Klavier (n)	piano
Kollegin (f)	female colleague
Kreis (m)	circle
Kursus (m)	course
Mitternacht (f)	midnight
Mittagspause (f)	lunch break
Mußestunde (f)	spare, relaxed hour
Priorität (f)	priority
Privatleben (n)	private life
Radiosendung (f)	radio programme
Reihenhaus (n)	terrace
Reinigung (f)	here: cleaners (of garments) (also: cleaning)
Schlaf (m)	sleep
Selbstständige (pl)	self-employed (people)
Selbsttest (m)	self-test
Sorge (f)	the worry
Streit (m)	row, argument
Tabelle (f)	table
Tasse (f)	cup
Trompete (f)	trumpet
Umsatz (m)	turnover
Vergnügung (f)	enjoyment (also: entertainment)
Verpflichtung (f)	duty
Vollzeit (f)	full-time
Wetter (n)	weather
Zeit (f)	time
Zeitunglesen (n)	(the) reading (of) the paper

Adjectives

blond	blonde
realistisch	realistic
schwarz	black
unrealistisch	unrealistic
wütend	angry

Verbs

absagen	to cancel
erholen	to recover
fehlen	to be missing
meditieren	to meditate
sammeln	to collect
verbessern	to improve

Adverbs

heutzutage	nowadays

Phrases

den hohen Anforderungen (nicht) gewachsen sein	to be up (or not) to the demands of the job
der ständige Ärger	permanent problems
im Ausland	abroad
im Griff haben	to be on top of something
körperliche Bewegung	physical exercis
pensioniert sein	to be a pension

LOOKING FORWARD

In Unit 10, we will consolidate what we have covered in the previous nine units. For the *Looking Forward* task this time, try to work out what this website is about:

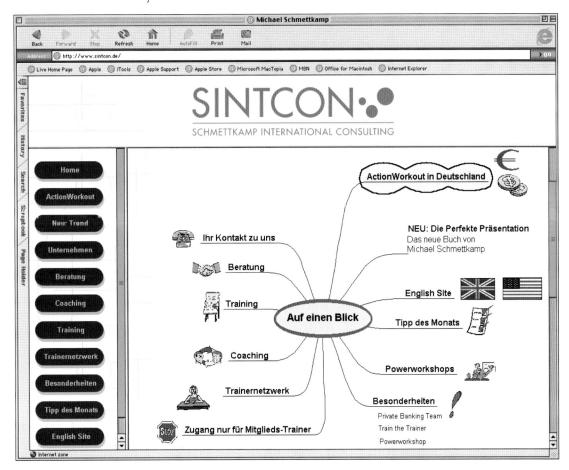

Who, in your opinion, would be searching this website? What information can you expect to find?

Try and use some of this vocabulary:

- Wahrscheinlich …
- Ich glaube, daß …
- Ich denke, daß …

Die Work-Life-Balance im 21. Jahrhundert

UNIT 10
Das Internet

In this unit, we will revise and consolidate much of what you have been studying throughout the course. This process of consolidation will help you to take your study of German further.

Specifically, you will revise and consolidate:
- Hypothesis and comparison (**würde**)
- Sentence connectors (**aber, weil**)
- Imperatives
- Techniques and strategies for oral discussion on other opinions.

You will learn and practise the use of:
- The correct forms of **wer** (**wer, wen, wem**)
- Possessive pronouns.

You will learn about:
- The cultural phenomenon of 'Denglish'
- How the technological revolution is influencing modern German life and the German language.

We suggest that you come back to this checklist as you progress through the unit. You can then judge how you are getting on.

1 Wissen Sie noch?

A Wie heissen die Sätze richtig?

Don't forget to capitalise the first letter of the first word in the sentence.

1 • gern möchte in keinen Paß ich Italien arbeiten, aber ich im Sommer habe noch

2 • Examen Daniel hat bestanden seine und wird im studieren September in Dresden

3 • die fahren Touristen vom Stadtzentrum Flughafen mit dem Bus ins, und Reisebegleiter der ins Hotel bringt sie dann

4 • Ben hat Ferienjob jetzt einen, weil er das braucht Geld für Semester das neue

5 • wir Tage wollen Potsdam ein paar in bleiben, buchen aber wir Hotel können kein

6 • Viele krank Mitarbeiter sind im zweimal Jahr, weil Urlaub sie nicht nehmen genug

B **Weil** oder **aber**?

1 • Ich würde gern eine Weltreise machen, ⟨ ⟩ ich habe nicht genug Geld.

2 • ⟨ ⟩ er ausgezeichnete Qualifikationen hat, hat Frank die Stelle bekommen.

3 • Sabine möchte keine Sahne, ⟨ ⟩ sie gerade eine Diät macht.

4 • Ahmed ist Arzt von Beruf, ⟨ ⟩ im Moment arbeitet er als Krankenpfleger.

5 • ⟨ ⟩ gut ist das nicht!

6 • Wir müssen leider einen Monat auf das neue Sofa warten, ⟨ ⟩ es momentan nicht auf Lager ist.

Das Internet

2 Was gehört zusammen?

A Lesen Sie und hören Sie die beiden Texte, und entscheiden Sie dann, welche Überschrift zu welchem Artikel gehört. Die Schlüsselwörter können Ihnen dabei helfen.

Überschrift 1: Internet am Arbeitsplatz
Überschrift 2: Unternehmen rüsten gegen E-Mail-Flut

Schlüsselwörter

der Nutzer	*user*
das Ergebnis	*result*
die Mehrheit	*majority*
beruflich bedingt	*to do with the job*
verschicken	*to send*
die geschäftliche Korrespondenz	*business correspondence*
erwünscht	*desired*
durchführen	*to conduct*

a

Jeder siebte Internet-Nutzer (14 Prozent), der das Web auch beruflich nutzt, verbringt täglich mehr als eine Stunde mit privatem Surfen am Arbeitsplatz. Dies ist das Ergebnis einer internetrepräsentativen Umfrage, die von Forsa durchgeführt wurde. Danach gehört für die Mehrheit der Surfer (57 Prozent) das Web zum Arbeitsalltag. Gut ein Drittel davon (34 Prozent) verbringt täglich bis zu 15 Minuten mit beruflich bedingtem Surfen. Weitere 44 Prozent surfen berufsbedingt zwischen 15 Minuten und einer Stunde.

b

Die E-Mail-Nutzung wird in den kommenden Jahren stark zunehmen, so lautet das Fazit des Annual E-Mail Usage Forecast von IDC. Die Marktforscher gehen davon aus, daß im Jahr 2005 pro Tag durchschnittlich 36 Mrd. E-Mails verschickt werden. Die Anzahl jener Menschen, die ein E-Mail-Postfach haben, wird von 505 Mio. im Jahr 2000 auf 1,2 Mrd. im Jahr 2005 steigen. Neben der erwünschten elektronischen Korrespondenz wird der Anteil von unerwünschter Werbe-Mail auf bis zu 50 Prozent steigen. Unternehmen in Deutschland und Österreich, die derzeit zu rund 80 Prozent E-Mail für ihre geschäftliche Korrespondenz nutzen, suchen verstärkt nach Lösungen, um die zu erwartende Datenflut in den Griff zu bekommen. Ein praktikabler E-Mail-Filter könnte diesbezüglich Abhilfe schaffen – so IDC.

B Ⓐ🅒 Lesen Sie die beiden Texte noch einmal und entscheiden Sie dann, ob die Sätze richtig oder falsch sind.

Richtig Falsch

1. One in seven people using the Internet at work also surfs for private purposes at work.

2. They spend up to 23 hours per working day surfing for non-work-related information.

3. Forty-four per cent use the Internet to search for job-related information for between 15 minutes and one hour.

4. Only 34 per cent of employees think the Internet is part of their professional routine.

5. Research predicts that, by 2005, 36 million e-mails will be sent per day.

6. In 2000, 505 million people had an e-mail address.

7. In 2005, 1.2 billion people will have an e-mail address.

8. At the same time, 'spam' is expected to rise by up to 50%.

LANGUAGE FOCUS

The two texts on the previous page show a phenomenon that is acknowledged in the German-speaking world as growing ever faster: 'Denglish' is becoming the rule. In no other area of society is this more evident than in the world of telecommunications. The phenomenal pace of technological development in this industry has had an effect on the volume of British and American terms being assimilated into German.

Sometimes a word or phrase is absorbed without any changes, e.g. **E-mail, die Mail, last-minute**. Other examples show words or phrases are taken over where part already existed in German, thus simplifying the allocation of an article, e.g. **die Work-Life-Balance (die Balance)**. Verbs are often taken from the English with the addition of a German verb ending, e.g. **surfen, mailen, shoppen**.

The reaction to such borrowing is mixed, but on the whole it is not very positive. However, discussions often disregard the fact that all language evolves, and throughout the centuries words from a number of languages have been assimilated into German, as they have into English.

3 Sie sind dran!

A Sehen Sie sich die Argumente an, und finden Sie dann Gegenargumente.

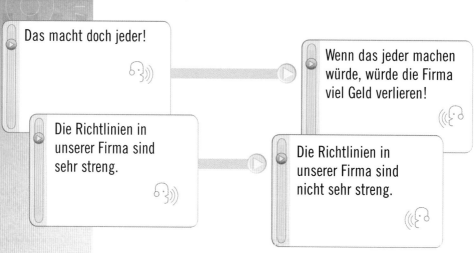

Das macht doch jeder!

Wenn das jeder machen würde, würde die Firma viel Geld verlieren!

Die Richtlinien in unserer Firma sind sehr streng.

Die Richtlinien in unserer Firma sind nicht sehr streng.

B Diskutieren Sie: Surfen Sie im Job auch privat?

Ja, weil …   Nein, weil …

Im Schüttelkasten finden Sie einige Vokabeln, die bei der Diskussion helfen könnten.

Schüttelkasten

**Die Richtlinien in der Firma
sind streng/nicht so streng.**

Das macht doch jeder!

Wenn das jeder machen würde, …

Das kostet doch nicht viel.

**Ich arbeite in einem
Großraumbüro, da können wir …**

4 Was fehlt hier?

  Ergänzen Sie die korrekten Präpositionen.

> **mit   für   in   in   zwischen   mit**

1 • Bei uns (⟶⟶⟶⟶) der Firma sind die Richtlinien sehr streng.

2 • Ich arbeite (⟶⟶⟶⟶) einem Großraumbüro.

3 • Die meisten Firmen nutzen rund 80% E-mail (⟶⟶⟶⟶) ihre
Korrespondenz.

4 • (⟶⟶⟶⟶) der erwünschten elektronischen Korrespondenz
steigt der Anteil an Werbe-Mail.

5 • Ein Drittel der Mitarbeiter verbringt jeden Tag ca. 30 Minuten
(⟶⟶⟶⟶) Internet-Surfen.

6 • Die anderen zwei Drittel surfen (⟶⟶⟶⟶) 30 Minuten und
einer Stunde.

5 Was würden Sie machen?

Spielen Sie in der Gruppe ein Wunsch-Spiel. This
game could probably be called the opposite of a reality show! Write
down a question on one piece of paper, and the answer on another.
Then mix up the two piles and create new pairs.

Beispiel:

Ich würde eine Weltreise
machen.

Ich würde gute Politik
machen.

Was würden Sie machen,
wenn Sie Premierminister
wären?

Was würden Sie machen,
wenn Sie im Lotto
gewinnen würden?

Wer hat die originellsten Paare?

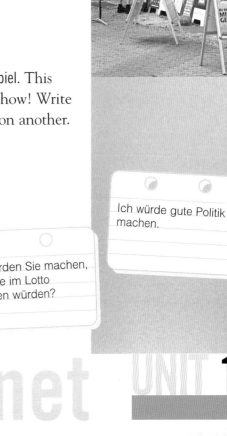

Das Internet

6 Was wäre, wenn …?

   Arbeiten Sie mit Ihrem Partner. Diskutieren Sie diese Idee:

Was würden Sie machen, wenn jeder Tag nicht 24, sondern 32 Stunden hätte?

Wenn ich mehr Zeit hätte, würde ich …

- mehr arbeiten
- mehr Zeit mit den Kindern verbringen
- mehr im Garten arbeiten
- öfter ins Theater gehen
- mehr verreisen
- mehr lesen
- mehr zu Hause sein

Wenn Sie Ihre Ideen diskutiert haben, erzählen Sie der Klasse, was Ihr Partner machen würde.

- Er würde …
- Sie würde …

As a subject question word, **wer** is straightforward and you are already familiar with its use:

- **Wer** ist dein Sohn?
- **Wer** ist Herr Schneider?
- **Wer** kommt denn da?

Wer can also be used in the accusative when the person in question is an accusative object:

- **Wen** möchten Sie sprechen?
- **Wen** kennen Sie?

Or when a preposition which takes the accusative is used:

- Über **wen** haben Sie gesprochen?
- Durch **wen** haben Sie das gehört?

If a preposition requiring the dative is used, **wer** becomes **wem**:

- Mit **wem** haben Sie gesprochen?

7 Sie sind dran!

Wer, wen oder *wem*? Fragen Sie nach der Information, die fettgedruckt ist.

Beispiel:

Frau Krause hat angerufen.
Wer hat angerufen?

1 • **Frau Krause** ist eine alte Kundin.

2 • **Sie** hat einen neuen OHP bestellt.

3 • Die Chefin hat selbst mit **ihr** gesprochen.

4 • **Sie** hat eine neue Telefonnummer.

5 • Die Chefin hat **sie** dann noch einmal angerufen.

6 • Sie hat einen Termin mit **ihr** vereinbart.

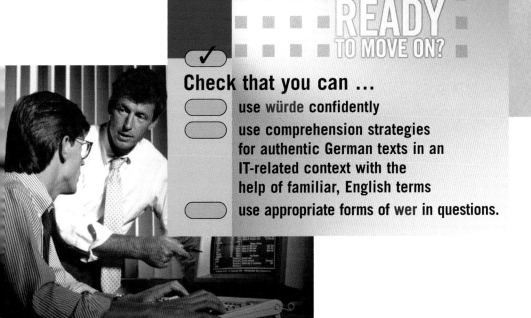

READY TO MOVE ON?

✓

Check that you can ...

- use **würde** confidently
- use comprehension strategies for authentic German texts in an IT-related context with the help of familiar, English terms
- use appropriate forms of **wer** in questions.

Das Internet UNIT **10**

8 Hören Sie mal!

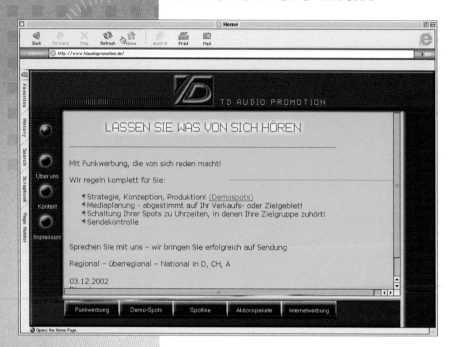

A  Hören Sie den Text. Es ist eine Anzeige aus dem Radio für ein bestimmtes Produkt.

Entscheiden Sie sich, für welches Produkt geworben wird:

- Trainingskurse
- Kinderwagen
- Kaufhaus
- Automodell
- Buggies

Schlüsselwörter

die Anzeige *advert*

 Was bedeutet das Wort 'Paradies'?

B Hören Sie jetzt die Anzeige noch einmal. Diskutieren Sie dann in der Klasse.

Was ist das Konzept, die Grundidee der Anzeige? Warum 'muß' man am Ende das Produkt kaufen?

Weil:

- man das Produkt/die Produkte zum Leben braucht
- das Produkt/die Produkte ein Statussymbol ist/sind
- das Produkt/die Produkte Luxus bedeutet/bedeuten
- das Produkt/die Produkte schön ist/sind
- das Produkt/die Produkte notwendig ist/sind
- man die Auswahl hat
- man dort gut einkaufen kann
- das Geschäft kinderfreundlich ist

C  Arbeiten Sie jetzt mit einem Partner und kreieren Sie eine Anzeige für ein Produkt Ihrer Wahl.

It really doesn't matter what product or service you choose. Just remember that your advert needs to be quite lively because it is intended for radio.

Im Schüttelkasten sind einige nützliche Wörter und Wortgruppen:

cool	einfach	revolutionär
	unersetzlich	neuartig
super	wunderschön	bedienungsfreundlich

9 Sicher im Internet einkaufen – wie funktioniert das?

Das ist der Titel des Textes auf der nächsten Seite:

UND SCHNELLER BEZAHLEN FINDEN SICHERER

Wie heißt der Titel korrekt?

A Bevor Sie den Text lesen, beantworten Sie bitte diese Frage in der ganzen Gruppe:

Was denken Sie, worum es in dem Text geht?

Es geht um:

- Internetseiten
- den Einkauf im Netz
- sichere Bezahlung
- neues Konsumverhalten.

Das Internet

B 🅰️ⓒ ✏️ ⏵ Lesen Sie jetzt den Text und finden Sie dann vier Tipps für den Einkauf im Internet mit Hilfe einer Suchmaschine.

Beispiel:

Geben Sie bei der Suche mehrere Wörter ein.

So arbeiten Suchmaschinen

Die Logik der Suchmaschinen ist relativ simpel: Sie verstehen oder interpretieren ihre Eingaben nicht, sondern listen die Seiten im Internet auf, auf denen der Begriff in der eingegebenen Schreibweise auftaucht.

Bessere Ergebnisse durch mehrere Wörter

Geben Sie bei der Suche mehrere Wörter ein. Sollen Wörter oder Begriffe in genau dieser Reihenfolge auftauchen, setzen Sie sie in Anführungszeichen.

Ein Beispiel

Wer Zimbeln (eine seltene Art von Musikinstrumenten) im Internet kaufen möchte, bekommt nach der Eingabe dieses Begriffs eine lange Liste aller möglichen Seiten, auf denen Informationen zu diesem Musikinstrument auftauchen. Ein Käufer sollte sich überlegen, welche Begriffe auf einer Seite vorkommen, die Zimbeln verkaufen. Beispielsweise: „Zimbel" und „Preis". Läßt er nun nach beiden Begriffen suchen, stößt er sofort auf einen Shop.

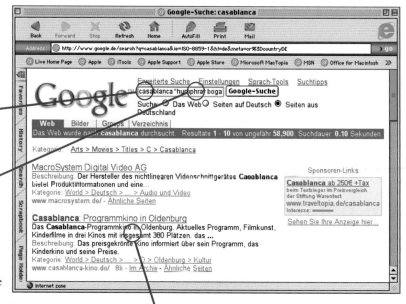

Die Priorisierung der Treffer

Es war lange Zeit ein Problem, in welcher sinnvollen Reihenfolge man beispielsweise 5.000 Treffer listet. Die Suchmaschine Google sortiert die Treffer nach ihrem Grade der Vernetzung. Je stärker eine Seite mit dem Internet vernetzt ist, desto weiter oben erscheint der Link auf der Liste. Denn was vielen Leuten einen Link wert ist, muß gut oder zumindest brauchbar sein, so die Überlegung der Google-Gründer Larry Page und Sergey Brin.

C 👥 🗣️ ⏵ Erzählen sie mal!

Tell your fellow students a story relating to one or more of the following questions:

- Haben Sie schon einmal im Internet eingekauft?
- Kaufen Sie oft im Internet ein?
- Was war Ihre beste Erfahrung?
- Ist schon einmal eine Katastrophe passiert?

LEARNING TIP:

For the imperative, put the verb in the infinitive form, followed by **Sie** for **Sie** sentences, and in the **du** form without the **-st** ending for **du** sentences, e.g.:

- Geben Sie zwei oder drei Wörter ein.
- Gib zwei oder drei Wörter ein.

LANGUAGE FOCUS

Possessive adjectives

Possessive adjectives, such as *your* or *his*, describe a noun in terms of possession and therefore do away with the need to use the same noun twice.

- Sabine sammelt CDs. Hier im Arbeitszimmer sind **ihre** CDs.

The choice of possessive adjective in German depends on the grammatical gender of the noun or subject in question. You first need to work out who the person 'in possession' in the sentence is, i.e. **ich = mein**. Secondly, you need to decide which gender the object is, i.e. Tasche ⟶ meine Tasche.

	ich	du	er/es	sie	wir	ihr	sie	Sie
masculine	mein	dein	sein	ihr	unser	euer	ihr	Ihr
feminine	meine	deine	seine	ihre	unsere	eure	ihre	Ihre
neuter	mein	dein	sein	ihr	unser	euer	ihr	Ihr
plural	meine	deine	seine	ihre	unsere	eure	ihre	Ihre

10 Wie heißt das richtig?

A Transform the following into possessive phrases.

Beispiel:

ich, Job ⟶ mein Job

1 • ich, Radio

2 • er, Computer

3 • wir, Haus

4 • Jutta, Kinder

5 • wir, Urlaub

6 • ich, Wochenende

7 • sie (singular), Adresse

8 • er, Auto

9 • sie (plural), Firma

10 • Bernd, Bücher

Das Internet

B [A C] ✍ ◐ Complete the missing possessive adjectives. Make sure you use the correct gender.

Beispiel:

Keith – das Segelboot   Das ist (**sein**) Segelboot.

1 • Jasmin – das Surfbrett   Das ist (   ) Surfbrett.

2 • Herr und Frau Schmidt –   Das ist (   ) Haus.
das Haus.

3 • Johannes – der Computer   Das ist (   ) Computer.

4 • Maria – das Baby   Das ist (   ) Baby.

5 • Ingrid – der Videorekorder   Das ist (   ) Videorekorder.

6 • Stavros – der Garten   Das ist (   ) Garten.

11 Was kann man hier machen?

Jetzt haben Sie sich durch das Buch *Access German* gearbeitet und sprechen schon gut deutsch!

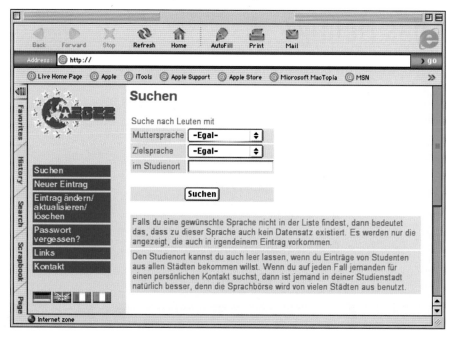

◖))) ◖◖ ◐ Sehen Sie sich bitte die Internetseite an. Was kann man hier machen? Arbeiten Sie mit einem Partner. Was möchten Sie machen? Was suchen Sie? Was können Sie bieten?

Was denken Sie, ist das eine gute Idee? Probieren Sie's mal!

GLOSSARY

Nouns

Anrufbeantworter (m)	answering machine
Anzeige (f)	advertisement
Arbeitsplatz (m)	work place
Erfahrung (f)	experience
Examen (n)	exam
Fax-Maschine (f)	fax machine
Fehler (m)	mistake
Flut (f)	flood
Großraumbüro (n)	open-plan office
Grundidee (f)	main idea
Konsumverhalten (n)	consumer behaviour
Katastrophe (f)	catastrophe
Korrespondenz (f)	correspondence
Krankenpfleger (m)	male nurse
Mitarbeiter (m)	member of staff
Paß (m)	passport
Qualifikation (f)	qualification
Reisebegleiter (m)	tour guide
Richtlinie (f)	guideline
Sahne (f)	cream
Segelboot (n)	sailing boat
Sofa (n)	sofa
Suchmaschine (f)	search engine
Unternehmen (n)	company
Videorekorder (m)	video recorder
Vokabeln (pl)	vocabulary
Weltreise (f)	trip around the world

Adjectives

bedienungsfreundlich	user-friendly
einfach	simple
elektronisch	electronic
neuartig	new (of a new type)
notwendig	necessary
revolutionär	revolutionary
streng	strict
unersetzlich	irreplaceable
wunderschön	very beautiful

Verbs

bestehen	to pass (exams)
surfen	to surf

Adverbs

momentan	currently

Das Internet

LANGUAGE SUMMARY

Gender and articles

There are three genders in German. All nouns are either masculine (**der**), feminine (**die**) or neuter (**das**). This distinction is not made in the plural.

The definite article (*the*) changes according to the gender of the noun, as does the indefinite article (*a/an*):

Gender	Definite article (*the*)	Indefinite article (*a/an*)
masculine	der	ein
feminine	die	eine
neuter	das	ein
plural	die	—

der Buch	*the book* (masculine)
eine Minute	*a minute* (feminine)
die Hobbys	*the hobbies* (plural)

As in English, there is no indefinite article in the plural.

The article refers only to the grammatical gender and has nothing to do with the natural gender of the noun. For instance, in German, 'girl' is not a feminine noun! It is **das Mädchen**, which is neuter.

ACCESS **GERMAN**

Plurals

The plural is usually formed by adding an ending to the singular. Masculine and neuter nouns often add an **–e** in the plural, whereas feminine nouns often form the plural by adding **–n** or **–en**. The following table will help you to form plurals:

Singular	+	Ending	=	Plural	Other examples
Banane		–n		Bananen	Salaten, Stücken, Adressen, Zitronen
Packung		–en		Packungen	Flaschen, Dosen, Erbsen, Tomaten, Weintrauben, Kartoffeln, Forellen, Orangen, Tassen
Brot		–e		Brote	Jahre, Pferde
Glas		*umlaut* + –er		Gläser	Männer, Häuser, Dächer
Ei		–er		Eier	Kleider, Bilder
Joghurt		–s		Joghurts	Schampoos, Kaffees, Autos
Waschmittel		—		Waschmittel	Fleisch, Würstchen, Käse, Schinken

Adjectives

Adjectives are words that describe a noun: **Der Wein ist *kalt*** (*The wine is cold*).

As in English, an adjective can also come before the noun it is describing: **der kalte Wein** (*the cold wine*). In this case, the adjective varies slightly, depending on the gender of the noun and its position in the sentence, usually adding an **-e** or an **-en**. However, these changes are complicated and it is easier at first to remember each phrase or sentence individually.

Comparatives

When comparing two or more nouns, the adjectives are compared, too.

Robert ist groß.   Michael ist größer.   Simon ist am größten.
Wein A ist kalt.   Wein B ist kälter.   Wein C ist am kältesten.

These are called the comparative (equivalent of *–er/more…*) and the superlative (equivalent of *–est/most …*).

Adjective	Comparative	Superlative
schön	schöner	am schönsten
reich	reicher	am reichesten
klein	kleiner	am kleinsten
rund	runder	am rundesten
lieb	lieber	am liebsten

Adjectives of one syllable with an **a**, **o** or **u** take an umlaut:

warm	wärmer	am wärmsten
dumm	dümmer	am dümmsten
kalt	kälter	am kältesten
alt	älter	am ältesten
groß	größer	am größten

Some adjectives are irregular, as they are in English (*good – better – best*):

gut	besser	am besten
nah	näher	am nächsten
viel	mehr	am meisten

When comparing two nouns directly, **als** is used.

Michael ist größer als Robert.	*Michael is bigger than Robert.*
Das Buch ist dicker als die Zeitung.	*The book is thicker than the newspaper.*
In München ist es kälter als in Berlin.	*In Munich it is colder than in Berlin.*

Cases

German nouns have four grammatical cases – nominative, accusative, dative and genitive, depending on their position and function in a sentence. Sometimes the article (*the* or *a*) will change, and occasionally the word will have an additional ending.

Nominative case

The nominative case is used for the subject of the sentence. A noun will generally be nominative if there is no reason for it *not* to be.

Accusative case

The accusative case is used for the object of a sentence and after certain prepositions (see *Prepositions* on page 176). The accusative case in German changes masculine articles, but not feminine or neuter articles.

	Definite articles		Indefinite articles	
	Nominative	**Accusative**	**Nominative**	**Accusative**
Masculine	der	den	ein	einen
Feminine	die	die	eine	eine
Neuter	das	das	ein	ein
Plural	die	die	—	—

	Subject	Verb	Direct object	
Masculine	Peter	kauft	ein**en** Lachs.	*Peter buys a salmon.*
Feminine	Meine Mutter	trinkt	eine Limonade.	*My mother drinks lemonade.*
Neuter	Ich	kaufe	ein Auto.	*I buy a car.*
Plural	Yussuf	hat	viele Katzen.	*Yussuf has a lot of cats.*

Dative case

The dative case is used for the *indirect object* and after certain prepositions (see *Prepositions* on page 176). The table below shows the changes in comparison with the nominative.

	Definite articles		Indefinite articles	
	Nominative	Dative	Nominative	Dative
Masculine	der	dem	ein	einem
Feminine	die	der	eine	einer
Neuter	das	dem	ein	einem
Plural	die	den	—	—

	Subject	Verb	Preposition	Indirect object
Masculine	Franz	wohnt	mit	seinem Vater.
Feminine	Lisa	schwimmt	seit	letzter Woche.
Neuter	Martina	geht	nach	ihrem Haus.
Plural	Die Babys	essen	mit	Ihre Händen.

Genitive case

The genitive case is used for possession. This case is not covered in detail in this course, but can generally be recognised by the **–es** added to masculine and neuter articles and nouns.

Pronouns and possessive adjectives

Personal pronouns

	Nominative	Accusative	Dative
I/me	ich	mich	mir
you (familiar, singular)	du	dich	dir
he/him, it	er	ihn	ihm
she/her, it	sie	sie	ihr
it, he/him, she/her	es	es	ihm
we/us	wir	uns	uns
you (plural)	ihr	euch	euch
you (polite, singular & plural)	Sie	Sie	Ihnen
they/them	sie	sie	ihnen

Sie is the formal way of addressing someone, whereas **du** is more informal. Even though conventions are relaxing in Germany, it is worth remembering that it is always safer to use **Sie** rather than **du**.

Possessive adjectives

Possessive adjectives, such as *your* or *his*, describe a noun in terms of possession and therefore do away with the need to use the same noun twice either in one sentence or in two successive sentences.

The choice of possessive adjective depends on the grammatical gender of the noun or subject in question. You need to think first who the person 'in possession' in the sentence is, i.e. **ich** becomes **mein**. And secondly you need to decide which gender you're using, i.e. **Tasche — meine Tasche**.

	ich	du	er/es	sie	wir	ihr	sie	Sie
Masculine	mein	dein	sein	ihr	unser	euer	ihr	Ihr
Feminine	meine	deine	seine	ihre	unsere	eure	ihre	Ihre
Neuter	mein	dein	sein	ihr	unser	euer	ihr	Ihr
Plural	meine	deine	seine	ihre	unsere	eure	ihre	Ihre

Prepositions

Prepositions are notoriously difficult to translate literally. It helps to memorise them in context.

Some prepositions need to be followed by an article in the accusative or dative case. There is also a group that can be followed by either case.

Prepositions taking the accusative case

durch	*through*
für	*for*
gegen	*against*
ohne	*without*
um	*around*
entlang	*along*

Prepositions taking the dative case

bei	*by*
mit	*with*
außer	*except*
bei	*at*
nach	*after*
seit	*since*
von	*from*
zu	*to*
aus	*from (places), out of (containers)*
gegenüber	*opposite*

Wechselpräpositionen *(alternating prepositions)*

These prepositions can take either the accusative or dative case, depending on their use in a sentence. This sounds more complicated than it is: the main difference is that when a sense of movement is conveyed, the accusative case is used, and when it is position or location, the dative case is used:

Die Mutter geht in **die** Küche.	movement = accusative	*The mother goes into the kitchen.*
Die Mutter ist in **der** Küche.	position = dative	*The mother is in the kitchen.*

The following prepositions can take either case:

an	*on, at, to*
in	*in, into*
auf	*on, onto*
unter	*under, beneath, below*
neben	*beside, next to*
vor	*in front of, before*
hinter	*behind*
zwischen	*between, in between*
über	*over, above*

When using the prepositions **an** and **bei** with neuter and masculine nouns, they are combined with the article:

an	+	dem	=	am
bei	+	dem	=	beim
in	+	dem	=	im

The preposition **zu** with masculine, neuter and feminine nouns also combines with the article:

zu	+	der	=	zur
zu	+	dem	=	zum

'to'

In order to express the notion of going 'to' a place, there are several options in German. Which one you choose will depend on whether the place in question is a town/country, a region, a place by the sea, etc.

	Wir fahren ...
Country, town, city	**nach** Spanien, **nach** London, **nach** Stafford, **nach** Cornwall.
Place in the mountains	**in** die Alpen, **in** die Dolomiten, **in** die Rocky Mountains.
Place by the water	**an** die Ostsee, **an** das Schwarze Meer, **an** den Nil.
Region	**in** den Lake District, **in** die Berge, **in** den Schwarzwald.

LANGUAGE SUMMARY

Word order

The main rule of German word order is that the main verb comes second. This does not necessarily mean that the verb is actually the second word, but that the verb is the second meaningful unit in the sentence. In first place we often put the word or phrase that carries the main emphasis of the sentence:

Ich trinke jeden Tag zwei Liter Wasser. ⎫
Zwei Liter Wasser trinke ich jeden Tag. ⎬ *I drink two litres of water every day.*

When describing an activity such as playing sports, the verb usually comes with another word, i.e. *to play football, to play tennis,* etc. In German, these constructions are split up; the verb goes in second position and the other word (usually a noun) goes to the end of the clause. This gives the speaker the opportunity to vary the meaning of the sentence so that the phrase at the front of the sentence carries more emphasis.

Ich spiele Fußball.   *I play football.*
Jeden Sonntag spiele ich Fußball. ⎫
Ich spiele jeden Sonntag Fußball. ⎬ *I play football every Sunday.*

If a sentence contains an additional (subordinate) clause, the verb goes to the end:

Ich würde gern im Ausland leben, weil das Wetter besser **ist**.
I would like to live abroad, because the weather is better.

See also the sections on Modal verbs, Separable verbs and the Perfect tense.

Verbs: present tense

Regular verbs

	kommen	*to come*
ich	komm**e**	*I come*
du	komm**st**	*you* (familiar) *come*
er/sie/es	komm**t**	*he/she/it comes*
Sie/wir/sie	komm**en**	*you* (polite) */we/they come*
ihr	komm**t**	*you* (familiar, plural) *come*

Some verbs have a vowel change in the middle when the **–st** and **–t** endings are added:

	fahren	*to go, to drive*
ich	fahre	*I go*
du	fährst	*you* (familiar) *go*
er/sie/es	fährt	*he/she/it goes*
Sie/wir/sie	fahren	*you* (polite) */we/they go*
ihr	fährt	*you* (familiar, plural) *go*

Irregular verbs

	sein	*to be*
ich	bin	*I am*
du	bist	*you (familiar) are*
er/sie/es	ist	*he/she/it is*
Sie/wir/sie	sind	*you (polite) /we/they are*
ihr	seid	*you (familiar, plural) are*

	haben	*to have*
ich	habe	*I have*
du	hast	*you (familiar) have*
er/sie/es	hat	*he/she/it has*
Sie/wir/sie	haben	*you (polite) /we/they have*
ihr	habt	*you (familiar, plural) have*

Modal verbs

There are six modal verbs: **müssen** (*must*), **wollen** (*want*), **dürfen** (*to be allowed*), **können** (*can, to be able to, to have permission*), **mögen** (*would like*) and **sollen** (*should*).

	wollen	**können**	**mögen**	**dürfen**	**müssen**	**sollen**
ich	will	kann	möchte	darf	muß	soll
du	willst	kannst	möchtest	darfst	mußt	sollst
er/sie/es	will	kann	möchte	darf	muß	soll
Sie/wir/sie	wollen	können	möchten	dürfen	müssen	sollen
ihr	wollt	könnt	möchtet	dürft	müsst	sollt

When a modal verb is used, the second verb always goes to the end.

Ich **will** im Sommer zwei Wochen **verreisen**.
I want to travel for two weeks in the summer.

Bernard **kann** tolle Präsentationen **entwerfen**.
Bernard can draw up great presentations.

Jacob ist erst neun Jahre alt. Er **darf** den Film noch nicht **sehen**.
Jacob is only nine years old. He is not allowed to see the film yet.

The modal verb is used in the form corresponding to the subject of the sentence, and the verb at the end is used in the infinitive ('to' form).

Separable verbs

Some verbs come in two parts, i.e. **fernsehen** = **sehen** + **fern** (*see* + *far*). When these are used in a sentence, the main part of the verb goes in second position, and the other bit is sent to the end. Very often this 'bit' is a preposition which, when added to a verb, changes the meaning of the verb:

kaufen	*to buy*
einkaufen	*to shop*
abkaufen	*to buy off (someone)*

If there is nothing to follow in the sentence, the main verb comes after the subject, and the preposition or other function is split up from it:

einkaufen	ich kaufe ein	*I shop*
radfahren	wir fahren Rad	*we cycle*
fernsehen	er sieht fern	*he watches TV*

See also the section on the Imperative, below.

Imperative

The imperative form is used for giving instructions or directions. There are two different forms, depending on whether you are familiar with the person you are talking to or not.

Sie form

The verb comes first in the sentence, then **Sie**:

Gehen Sie nach rechts.	*Go to the right.*
Nehmen Sie die erste Straße links.	*Take the first street on the left.*
Fahren Sie nach München.	*Go to Munich.*

du form

When addressing someone as **du**, e.g. a child or someone with whom you are on familiar terms, the imperative is formed by removing the **–st** from the **du** verb form and then losing the word **du**:

| du gehst | ⟶ | geh | *go* |
| du nimmst | ⟶ | nimm | *take* |

There are no umlauts (**ü, ä, ö**) in the imperative:

| du fährst | ⟶ | fahr |

Geh nach rechts.
Nimm die erste Straße links.
Fahr nach München.

For separable verbs, the prefix is split from the main part of the verb and sent to the end:

| aufstehen *(to get up)* | ⟶ | Stehen Sie auf. |
| zuhören *(to listen closely)* | ⟶ | Hören Sie zu. |

Perfect tense

The perfect tense is used to express events in the past and is used exclusively in spoken German for that purpose. It is also increasingly used in written German to express something that happened in the past.

The past is formed by using **haben** or **sein** + past participle:

Ich habe studiert.   *I (have) studied.*

The past participle most commonly ends in **–en** or **–t** and often starts with **ge–**. However, there are many variations, and each should be individually learnt.

kommen ——► gekommen
trinken ——► getrunken
studieren ——► studiert

The auxiliary verb (**haben** or **sein**) in the appropriate form goes in second position and the past participle is last.

Nach der Schule habe ich Germanistik studiert.   *I did German Studies after I left school.*

Wir haben gestern zwei Filme gesehen.   *We saw two films yesterday.*

Most verbs use **haben** to form their past participle. The following list shows the most important verbs that use **sein** rather than **haben**:

fahren	*drive*
fallen	*fall*
fliegen	*fly*
gehen	*go*
geschehen	*happen*
kommen	*come*
laufen	*run*
passieren	*happen*
reisen	*travel*
rennen	*run, race*
schwimmen	*swim*
sein	*be*
springen	*jump*
verschwinden	*disappear*
wachsen	*grow*
werden	*become*

Past participles of verbs

abfahren	**abgefahren**	fragen	**gefragt**	saubermachen	**saubergemacht**
abholen	**abgeholt**	freuen	**gefreut**	schließen	**geschlossen**
absagen	**abgesagt**	genießen	**genossen**	schreiben	**geschrieben**
ankommen	**angekommen**	geschehen	**geschehen**	schwimmen	**geschwommen**
arbeiten	**gearbeitet**	haben	**gehabt**	sein	**gewesen**
aufmachen	**aufgemacht**	heiraten	**geheiratet**	spielen	**gespielt**
backen	**gebacken**	heißen	**geheißen**	springen	**gesprungen**
beginnen	**begonnen**	hören	**gehört**	stricken	**gestrickt**
besichtigen	**besichtigt**	kennenlernen	**kennengelernt**	studieren	**studiert**
bestehen	**bestanden**	kochen	**gekocht**	surfen	**gesurft**
bestellen	**bestellt**	kommen	**gekommen**	tanzen	**getanzt**
besuchen	**besucht**	kosten	**gekostet**	trinken	**getrunken**
bezahlen	**bezahlt**	lesen	**gelesen**	übernachten	**übernachtet**
brauchen	**gebraucht**	machen	**gemacht**	umsteigen	**umgestiegen**
einkaufen	**eingekauft**	meditieren	**meditiert**	verbessern	**verbessert**
einladen	**eingeladen**	mieten	**gemietet**	verkaufen	**verkauft**
enthalten	**enthalten**	mieten	**gemietet**	verordnen	**verordnet**
ergänzen	**ergänzt**	nachsehen	**nachgesehen**	verreisen	**verreist**
erholen	**erholt**	nähen	**genäht**	verschwinden	**verschwunden**
erraten	**erraten**	nehmen	**genommen**	wachsen	**gewachsen**
erreichen	**erreicht**	organisieren	**organisiert**	wählen	**gewählt**
essen	**gegessen**	passieren	**passiert**	wandern	**gewandert**
fahren	**gefahren**	planen	**geplant**	werden	**geworden**
fallen	**gefallen**	recherchieren	**recherchiert**	wohnen	**gewohnt**
fehlen	**gefehlt**	rennen	**gerannt**	zuhören	**zugehört**
fernsehen	**ferngesehen**	sammeln	**gesammelt**		

Hypothetical sentences

Ich würde gern/lieber ...	*I'd rather…*
Ich hätte gern/lieber ...	*I'd rather have…*

ich	würde	hätte
du	würdest	hättest
er/sie/es	würde	hätte
Sie/wir/sie	würden	hätten
ihr	würdet	hättet

The two parts of the sentences below are linked with **aber** (*but*), and in the second part **würde** or **hätte** is used to express something hypothetical or something you would rather have. The second verb (in the infinitive) goes to the end of the sentence.

Wir fahren in August nach Bayern, aber ich würde lieber nach Griechenland fahren.
We're going to Bavaria in August, but I'd rather go to Greece.

Ich arbeite in Hamburg, aber ich würde lieber in Berlin arbeiten.
I work in Hamburg, but I'd rather work in Berlin.

Ich habe zwei Kinder, aber ich hätte gern sieben!
I have two children, but I'd rather have seven!

wer *(who/whom)*

As a subject question word, **wer** is straightforward:

Wer ist dein Sohn? *Who is your son?*

Wer becomes **wen** in the accusative:

Wen möchten Sie sprechen? *Who(m) do you want to speak to?*
Durch wen haben Sie das gehört? *From who(m) did you hear that?*

In the dative, **wer** becomes **wem**:

Mit wem haben Sie gesprochen? *With who(m) did you speak?*

Numbers

1	eins	11	elf	21	einundzwanzig
2	zwei	12	zwölf	22	zweiundzwanzig
3	drei	13	dreizehn	29	neunundzwanzig
4	vier	14	vierzehn	30	dreißig
5	fünf	15	fünfzehn	40	vierzig
6	sechs	16	sechzehn	50	fünfzig
7	sieben	17	siebzehn	60	sechzig
8	acht	18	achtzehn	70	siebzig
9	neun	19	neunzehn	80	achtzig
10	zehn	20	zwanzig	90	neunzig
				100	(ein)hundert

Cardinal numbers

erste	*first*
zweite	*second*
dritte	*third*

From the fourth cardinal number, **–te** is added to the ordinal number:

vier**te**	*fourth*
fünf**te**	*fifth*
sechs**te**	*sixth*

Days of the week

Montag	*Monday*	All days are masculine (**der**).
Dienstag	*Tuesday*	
Mittwoch	*Wednesday*	Am Dienstag gehe ich schwimmen. *On Tuesday I go swimming.*
Donnerstag	*Thursday*	Am Mittwoch mache ich Aerobic. *On Wednesday I do aerobics.*
Freitag	*Friday*	
Samstag	*Saturday*	
Sonntag	*Sunday*	

LANGUAGE SUMMARY

Time

In Germany, the 24-hour clock is used very frequently.

17.00 Uhr	siebzehn Uhr
17.45 Uhr	siebzehn Uhr fünfundvierzig

The 12-hour clock is very similar to English:

vor	*to*
nach	*past*

8.20	zwanzig nach acht
7.50	zehn vor acht
7.45	Viertel vor acht
8.15	Viertel nach acht

Uhr (*o'clock*) is not used.

When using the 12-hour clock, half the hour is half *before* the hour rather than half *past*.

9.30	halb zehn (*half ten*)
3.30	halb vier (*half four*)

GERMAN-ENGLISH WORDLIST

These word lists give the German words and phrases appearing in the course in alphabetical order (German–English and English–German), together with the unit number(s) in which they are presented.

A

aber	but	3
abfahren	to depart	4
abgeben	to hand in	3
Abflug (m)	flight departure	8
abgestorben	dead (wood)	6
abholen	to fetch (someone or something)	4
absagen	to cancel	9
Abteilungsleiter (m)	head of department	8
Adresse (f)	address	1
aktiv	active	1
amerikanisch	American	1
an	on, at	6, 7
Anblick (m)	view	6
Anfang (m)	beginning	8
angenehm	pleasant	1
Angenehm	Nice to meet you	1
Anglistik (f)	English studies	8
ankommen	to arrive	4
Ankunft (f)	arrival	8
Anrufbeantworter (m)	answering machine	10
Anwendung (f)	indication	7
Anzeige (f)	advertisement	10
Apfel (m)	apple	5
Apfelstrudel (m)	apple strudel	5

Apotheke (f)	chemist's, pharmacy	4
arbeiten	to work	2
Arbeitsmarkt (m)	job market	9
Arbeitsplatz (m)	work place	10
Argument (n)	argument	9
Assistentin (f)	(female) assistant	3
Arztpraxis (f)	doctor's surgery	4
Aubergine (f)	aubergine	5
auf	on (top), on (to)	7
auf dem Laufenden halten	to keep someone updated	7
auf seine Kosten kommen	to be worthwhile	6
Auf Wiedersehen!	Goodbye!	1
aufmachen	to open	8
Auge (n)	eye	6
aus	from (place)	7
Ausflug (m)	excursion	7
außer	apart from	7
Ausstellung (f)	exhibition	8
Auto (n)	car	4

B

Baby (n)	baby	1
backen	bake, to	5
Balkon (m)	balcony	9
Banane (f)	banana	5
Bank (f)	bank	2
Bauch (m)	stomach, belly	6

Bauchschmerzen (pl)	stomach ache	7
bedienungsfreundlich	user-friendly	10
beginnen	to start	2
bei	at	7
Bein (n)	leg	6
bequem	comfortable	4
Beruf (m)	profession	2
beruflich	on business	7
berühmt	famous	1, 2
Beschwerde (f)	complaint	7
besichtigen	to visit	6
bestehen	to pass (exams)	10
bestellen	to order	5
besuchen	to visit	2, 4
Bewerbung (f)	application	8
bezahlen	to pay	7
Bibliothek (f)	library	4
Bier (n)	beer	1, 5
Bild (n)	picture	2, 8
bitte	please	1
blond	blonde	9
Bratwurst (f)	sausages (fried)	5
brauchen	to need	4
Briefkasten (m)	postbox	4
Briefmarke (f)	postage stamp	4
Brokkoli (m)	broccoli	5
Brücke (f)	bridge	4

German	English	Unit
Brust (f)	breast	5
Buch (n)	book	2
Bundeskanzler (m)	Chancellor	2
Bushaltestelle (f)	bus stop	9
Butter (f)	butter	5

D

German	English	Unit
Dach (n)	roof	7
Dachdecker (m)	roofer	7
danke	thank you	1
Datenbank (f)	database	3
den hohen Anforderungen (nicht) gewachsen sein	be up (or not) to the demands of the job	9
Denkmal (n)	monument	4
Dessert (n)	dessert	5
deutsch	German	1
deutschsprachig	German-speaking	8
dick	thick, big	8
Dienstag (m)	Tuesday	3
Donnerstag (m)	Thursday	3
Dose (f)	tin	5
Drucker (m)	printer	8

E

German	English	Unit
ein bisschen	a little	3
einfach	simple	10
einkaufen	to shop	2, 4
einladen	to invite	6
Einzelhaus (n)	detached house	9
Eisen (n)	iron	9
elektronisch	electronic	10
Elternabend (m)	parents' evening	6
Empfang (m)	reception	5
englisch	English	1
enthalten	to contain	7
er	he	1
Erbse (f)	pea	5
Erdbeermarmelade (f)	strawberry jam	9
Erfahrung (f)	experience	10
Erfolg haben	to be successful	8
ergänzen	to complete	5
erholen	to recover	9
Erkältung (f)	cold	7
erraten	to guess	6
erreichen	to reach	6
essen	to eat	5

German	English	Unit
Etage (f)	floor (as in first, second, etc.)	4
Examen (n)	exam	10

F

German	English	Unit
fahren	to go (by car or train)	2
Fahrrad (n)	bicycle	6
Fahrscheinautomat (m)	ticket machine	4
Fahrt (f)	journey	8
fallen	to fall, to die (in action)	8
Familienname (m)	surname	1
Fasching (m)	carnival	3
Fax (n)	fax machine	10
fehlen	to be missing	9
fehlend	missing	8
Fehler (m)	fault, mistake	7, 10
Feierabend (m)	the time after work	9
Fenster (n)	window	5
Ferienwohnung (f)	holiday apartment	6
fernsehen	to watch TV	2
Fertiggericht (n)	convenience meal	5
Film (m)	film	2
Firma (f)	company	2
Fisch (m)	fish	5
Flasche (f)	bottle	5
Fleisch (n)	meat	5
Flug (m)	flight	4
Flughafen (m)	airport	4, 8
Fluß (m)	river	6
Flut (f)	flood	10
folgend	following	6
Forelle (f)	trout	5
Formular (n)	form	7
Fortbildungsinstitut (m)	training provider	5
fragen	to ask	5
Frau (f)	woman, wife, Mrs	1, 2
Freitag (m)	Friday	3
Freizeit (f)	spare time	9
Führungskraft (f)	senior manager	9
furchtbar	awful	7
Fuß (m)	foot	6
Fußball (m)	football	2

G

German	English	Unit
Galerie (f)	gallery	2, 4
Garten (m)	garden	4
Gebäude (n)	building	8
Geburtstag (m)	birthday, date of birth	7
Geburtstagskuchen (m)	birthday cake	6
Gefrierschrank (m)	freezer	8
gegenüber	opposite	7
Gemüse (n)	vegetables	5
genießen	to enjoy	4
Geld (n)	money	8
Germanistik (f)	German Studies	8
geschehen	to happen	8
griechisch	Greek	8
Grippe (f)	flu	7
Großraumbüro (n)	open-plan office	10
Grundidee (f)	main idea	10
Gut (n)	large farmstead	8
Guten Abend!	Good evening.	1
Guten Morgen!	Good morning.	1
Guten Tag!	Hello.	1
Gutshaus (n)	manor house	8

H

German	English	Unit
Haarwaschmittel (n)	shampoo	5
haben	to have	2
Hähnchen (n)	chicken	5
Halbinsel (f)	peninsula	6
Halsschmerzen (pl)	sore throat	7
Haltestelle (f)	station, stop	4
Handy (n)	mobile phone	9
Hauptgericht (n)	main course	5
Haus (n)	house	2
Hausbesuch (m)	(doctor's) home visit	7
Hausmann (m)	house husband	2
Hausnummer (f)	house number	4
Heimweh (n)	homesickness	9
heiraten	to get married	8
heißen	to be called	1
Hetzjagd (f)	chase	9
heute	today	3
heutzutage	formerly	9
Himbeere (f)	raspberry	5
hinter	behind	7

German	English	
Hobbys (pl)	hobbies	1
hoffentlich	hopefully	6
hören	to hear, to listen	2, 5
Hosenanzug (m)	trouser suit	9
Hotel (n)	hotel	4
Hunger haben	to be hungry	4

I

ich	I	1
im Ausland	abroad	9
im Garten arbeiten	to garden	2
im Griff haben	to be on top of something	9
in	in	6, 7
inlineskaten	to rollerblade	2
interessant	interesting	2
Internet surfen	to surf the Internet	1
ist schief gegangen	went wrong	7

J

Jakobsmuschel (f)	scallop	5
Jahr (n)	year	2, 6
Jahrhundert (n)	century	2, 8
jeden Tag	every day	3
Job (m)	job	3
Joghurt (m)	yoghurt	5
jung	young	1
Junker (m)	landed aristocrat	8

K

Kaffeekanne (f)	coffee pot	7
kalt	cold	8
Kantine (f)	canteen	9
Kartoffel (f)	potato	5
Käse (m)	cheese	5
Kastanienbaum (m)	horse chestnut tree	7
Kasten (m)	box	9
Katastrophe (f)	catastrophe	10
keine Zeit	no time	3
Kreme (f)	cream	5
Kate (f)	small farm worker's cottage	8
Kaufhaus (n)	department store	4

German	English	
Kaufhaus-Kette (f)	department-store chain	3
Kellner (m)	waiter (male)	5
Kellnerin (f)	waitress	5
kennenlernen	to meet	4
Kino (n)	cinema	3
Klavier (n)	piano	9
Klavier spielen	to play the piano	2
Kleid (n)	dress	8
klein	small, little	4
Kneipe (f)	pub	6
kochen	to cook	2, 5
Koffer (m)	suitcase	8
Kollegin (f)	female colleague	9
kommen	to come	1
Konferenz (f)	conference	5
Konsumverhalten (n)	consumer behaviour	10
Konzert (n)	concert	3
Konzertsaal (m)	concert hall	3
Kopfschmerzen (pl)	headache	7
Kormoran (m)	cormorant	6
körperliche Bewegung	physical exercise	9
Korrespondenz (f)	correspondence	10
kosten	to cost	5
Krabbe (f)	prawn	5
krank	ill	6
Krankenpfleger (m)	male nurse	10
Kreis (m)	circle	9
Kreme (f)	cream	5
Kursus (m)	course	9

L

Lachs (m)	salmon	5
langsam	slow	5
langweilig	boring	6
Laufbahn (f)	career	7
laut	noisy	4
Leben (n)	life	8
Lebenslauf (m)	CV, biography	8
Lehre (f)	apprenticeship	8
Lehrer (m)	teacher	2
leider	unfortunately	4
Leihwagen (m)	hire car	7

German	English	
lesen	to read	2
Lexikon (n)	dictionary, encyclopaedia	7
liebe Grüße	lots of love (to end a letter)	6
Limonade (f)	lemonade	5

M

machen	to make, to do	2
Maler (m)	painter	2
Mechaniker (m)	mechanic	8
meditieren	to meditate	9
Meer (n)	sea	6
merkwürdig	strange	6
mieten	to hire, to rent	6
Migräne (f)	migraine	4, 7
Milchprodukt (n)	dairy product	5
Mineralwasser (n)	mineral water	5
Minute (f)	minute	6
mit	with	5, 7
Mitarbeiter (m)	member of staff, colleague, employee	2, 10
Mittag (m)	midday, lunchtime	7
Mittagspause (f)	lunch break	9
Mitternacht (f)	midnight	9
Mittwoch (m)	Wednesday	3
momentan	currently	10
Montag (m)	Monday	3
Morgen (m)	morning	6
müde	tired	3
Museum (m)	museum	4
Musik (f)	music	1, 2
Müsli (n)	muesli	5
müssen (m)	must, to be able to	3
Mußestunde (f)	spare, relaxed hour	9
Mutter (f)	mother	1

N

nach	after	7
nach Hause	to (go) home	6
nachsehen	check, to	6
Nachspeise (f)	dessert	5
nähen	to sew	8
Name (m)	name	1

Nase *(f)*	nose	6
nass	wet	7
Naturfreund *(m)*	nature lover	6
neben	next to	7
nehmen	to take	4
neu	new	2, 4, 5
neuartig	new (of a new type)	10
Noch einmal, bitte.	Please repeat.	1
notwendig	necessary	10

O

Obst *(n)*	fruit	5
Ohr *(n)*	ear	6
Olive *(f)*	olive	5
Opernhaus *(n)*	opera house	4
Orange *(f)*	orange	5
Orangensaft *(m)*	orange juice	5
organisieren	to organise	8
Ort *(m)*	place village	6

P

Packung *(f)*	pack	5
Panne *(f)*	something wrong with a car, breakdown	4
Paradies *(n)*	paradise	6
Parkplatz *(m)*	parking space	4
Parkuhr *(f)*	parking meter	4
Paß *(m)*	passport	10
passieren	to happen	8
Patient *(m)*	patient	7
pensioniert sein	to be a pensioner	9
perfekt	perfect	6
Pfannkuchen *(m)*	pancake	6
Pferd *(m)*	horse	6
Pizzeria *(f)*	pizza restaurant	4
planen	to plan	8
Platz *(m)*	square	4
Politiker *(m)*	politician	2
Pommes frites	French fries	5
Postkarte *(f)*	postcard	4
Postleitzahl *(f)*	postcode	1
Premierminister *(m)*	prime minister	2
Priorität *(f)*	priority	9
Privatleben *(n)*	private life	9
Programmierer *(m)*	programmer	2
Projektbericht *(m)*	project report	3

Q

Qualifikation *(f)*	qualification	10

R

Radiosendung *(f)*	radio programme	9
Räucherschinken *(m)*	dry-cured ham	
realistisch	realistic	9
recherchieren	to research	6
Regenmantel *(m)*	raincoat	8
Regionalzug *(m)*	regional train	8
reich	rich	8
Reihe *(f)*	row, series	6
Reihenhaus *(n)*	terrace	9
Reinigung *(f)*	cleaners (of garments)	9
Reis *(m)*	rice	5
Reisebegleiter *(m)*	tour guide	10
Reiterhof *(m)*	farm offering horse-riding	6
rennen	to run	8
revolutionär	revolutionary	10
Rezept *(n)*	recipe	5
Richtlinie *(f)*	guideline	10
Richtung *(f)*	direction	4
Risotto *(m)*	risotto	5
Rolle *(f)*	role	2, 6
Rotwein *(m)*	red wine	5
Rückenschmerzen *(pl)*	backache	7
Rumpsteak *(n)*	rump steak	5

S

Sahne *(f)*	cream (double, single, etc.)	5, 10
sammeln	to collect	9
Samstag *(m)*	Saturday	3
Satz *(m)*	sentence	5
saubermachen	to clean	8
sauer	sour	8
Schalter *(m)*	counter	8
Schauspieler *(m)*	actor	2
Scheibe *(f)*	slice	5
Schinken *(m)*	ham	5
Schlaf *(m)*	sleep	9
Schlafstörung *(f)*	insomnia	7
Schlaftablette *(f)*	sleeping pill	7
Schlange *(f)*	queue	8

schlecht gelaunt sein	to be in a bad mood	7
schließen	to close	5
Schnupperangebot *(n)*	special offer	6
Schokoladenkreme *(n)*	chocolate mousse	5
schreiben	to write	5
Schule *(f)*	school	2
Schulter *(f)*	shoulder	6
schwarz	black	9
Schweinefilet *(n)*	pork fillet	5
Schweinebraten *(m)*	roast pork	5
schwimmen	to swim	1, 2
Segelboot *(n)*	sailing boat	10
Sehenswürdigkeit *(f)*	sight	6
sein	to be	1, 2
seit	since, for	7
Seite *(f)*	side, page	4
Sekretärin *(f)*	secretary	2
Selbständige *(pl)*	self-employed	9
Selbsttest *(m)*	self-test	9
Sender *(m)*	channel (TV or radio)	2
sich freuen auf	to look forward to	4
sich interessieren für	to be interested in	5
(sich) treffen	to meet	3
sich wenden an	to approach	7
Sie	you (polite)	1
sie	she	1
Sofa *(n)*	sofa	10
Sonnabend *(m)*	Saturday	3
Sonntag *(m)*	Sunday	3
Sorge *(f)*	worry	6, 9
Spargel *(m)*	asparagus	5
Speisekarte *(f)*	menu	5
spektakulär	spectacular	6
spielen	to play	1
springen	to jump	8
Stadtkirche *(f)*	(city) church	3
Stadtpark *(m)*	inner-city park	3
Staatsangehörigkeit *(f)*	nationality	1
Stammbaum *(m)*	family tree	8
Station *(f)*	station, stop	4
Stelle *(f)*	job, position	8

German	English	
Stock (m)	floor (as in first, second, etc.)	4
Straße (f)	street/road	2, 4, 6
Streit (m)	row	9
streng	strict	10
stricken	to knit	8
Stück (n)	piece	5
studieren	to study	3
Studium (n)	university course	8
Stunde (f)	hour	6
Suchmaschine (f)	search engine	10
Suppe (f)	soup	5
surfen	to surf	1, 10

T

German	English	
Tabelle (f)	table	9
Tablette (f)	pill	7
Tag (m)	day	3
Tagesdosis (f)	daily dose	7
tanzen	to dance	2
Tasche (f)	case, handbag	8
Tasse (f)	cup	9
Telefongespräch (n)	telephone conversation	7
Telefonnummer (f)	telephone number	2
Tennis (n)	tennis	1
Termin (m)	appointment	7
Theater (n)	theatre	1
Tisch (m)	table	5
Tischler (m)	carpenter	8
toll	great (slightly colloquial)	6
Touristeninformation (f)	tourist information	4
trinken	to drink	1, 5
Trockenpulver (n)	powder	7
Trompete (f)	trumpet	9
Tschüs!	See you!	1

U

German	English	
über	over, across	7
übernachten	to spend the night	7
Umsatz (m)	turnover	9

German	English	
umsteigen	to change (trains, planes, etc.)	4
unbedingt	absolutely, definitely	6
unbekannt	unknown	6
unersetzlich	irreplaceable	10
ungefähr	approximately	4
unhöflich	impolite	7
Universität (f)	university	4
unrealistisch	unrealistic	9
unter	under, underneath	7
Unternehmen (n)	company	10
Unterricht (m)	tuition	3
Urlaub (m)	holiday	6

V

German	English	
Vanilleeis (n)	vanilla ice-cream	5
Vater (m)	father	2
verbessern	to improve	9
Vergnügung (f)	enjoyment	9
verkaufen	to sell	4
verordnen	to prescribe	7
Verpflichtung (f)	duty	9
verreisen	to travel	6
verschwinden	to disappear	8
Videorekorder (m)	video recorder	10
viel zu tun haben	to have a lot to do	3
virtuell	virtual	2
Vogelliebhaber (m)	bird watcher	6
Vokabeln (pl)	vocabulary	10
vollberuflich (f)	full-time	3
von	from (time)	7
vor	in front of	7
Vorname (m)	first name	1
Vorspeise (f)	first course	5
Vortrag (m)	lecture	5

W

German	English	
wachsen	to grow	8
wählen	to choose	5
Wald (m)	woods	6
Wand (f)	wall	7
wandern	to walk	6
Waschmittel (n)	washing powder	5
Wechselgeld (n)	change	7
Wein (m)	wine	5

German	English	
Weintrauben	grapes	5
Weißkohl (m)	(white) cabbage	5
Weißwein (m)	white wine	5
weiter	further	6
Weizenbier (n)	wheat beer	5
Weltreise (f)	trip around the world	10
werden	to become	8
Werkstatt (f)	garage	4
Wetter (n)	weather	9
Wirkstoff (m)	active ingredient	7
wissen	to know	3
Wissen Sie noch?	Do you remember?	3
Woche (f)	week	2, 6
Wochenende (n)	weekend	7
wohnen	to live	1
wunderschön	wonderful, very beautiful	10
wütend	angry	9

Z

German	English	
Zahnschmerzen (pl)	toothache	7
Zeit (f)	time	9
Zeitungslesen (n)	(the) reading (of) the paper	9
zentral	central	4
Zielort (m)	destination	6
Zimmer (n)	room	4
Zimmernummer (f)	room number	7
Zitrone (f)	lemon	7
Zoo (m)	zoo	4
zu	to	7
zuerst	firstly	8
Zug (m)	train	4, 5
zu Hause	at home	3
zuhören	to listen	4
zukünftig	future	8
zur Abwechslung	for a change	6
zur Kenntnis bringen	to bring to attention	7
Zusammensetzung (f)	composition	7
zwischen	(in) between	7

GERMAN–ENGLISH WORDLIST

ENGLISH-GERMAN WORDLIST

A

abroad	im Ausland	9
absolutely	unbedingt	6
active	aktiv	1
active ingredient		
	Wirkstoff (m)	7
actor	Schauspieler (m)	2
address	Adresse (f)	1
advertisement	Anzeige (f)	10
after	nach	7
airport	Flughafen (m)	4, 8
American	amerikanisch	1
angry	wütend	9
answering machine		
	Anrufbeantworter (m)	10
apart from	außer	7
apple	Apfel (m)	5
apple strudel	Apfelstrudel (m)	5
application	Bewerbung (f)	8
appointment	Termin (m)	7
apprenticeship	Lehre (f)	8
approach, to	sich wenden an	7
approximately	ungefähr	4
argument	Argument (n)	9
arrival	Ankunft (f)	8
arrive, to	ankommen	4
ask, to	fragen	5
asparagus	Spargel (m)	5
assistant (female)		
	Assistentin (f)	3
at	bei	7
at home	zu Hause	3

aubergine	Aubergine (f)	5
awful	furchtbar	7

B

baby	Baby (n)	1
backache	Rückenschmerzen (pl)	7
bake, to	backen	5
balcony	Balkon (m)	9
banana	Banane (f)	5
bank	Bank (f)	2
be called, to	heißen	1
be hungry, to	Hunger haben	4
be in a bad mood, to	schlecht gelaunt sein	7
be interested in, to	sich interessieren für	5
be missing, to	fehlen	9
be a pensioner, to	pensioniert sein	9
be on top of something, to	im Griff haben	9
be successful, to	Erfolg haben	8
be worthwhile, to	auf seine Kosten kommen	6
be, to	sein	1, 2
become, to	werden	8
beer	Bier (n)	1, 5
beginning	Anfang (m)	8
behind	hinter	7
belly	Bauch (m)	6

between	zwischen	7
bicycle	Fahrrad (n)	6
bird watcher	Vogelliebhaber (m)	6
birthday	Geburtstag (m)	7
birthday cake	Geburtstagskuchen (m)	6
black	schwarz	9
blonde	blond	4
book	Buch (n)	2
boring	langweilig	6
bottle	Flasche (f)	5
box	Kasten (m)	9
breast	Brust (f)	5
bridge	Brücke (f)	4
bring to attention, to	zur Kenntnis bringen	7
broccoli	Brokkoli (m)	5
building	Gebäude (n)	8
bus stop	Bushaltestelle (f)	9
busy, to be	viel zu tun haben	3
but	aber	3
butter	Butter (f)	5

C

cancel, to	absagen	9
canteen	Kantine (f)	9
car	Auto (n)	4
career	Laufbahn (f)	7
carnival	Fasching (m)	3
carpenter	Tischler (m)	8
case	Tasche (f)	8
catastrophe	Katastrophe (f)	10

N

name	Name (m)	1
nature lover	Naturfreund (m)	6
necessary	notwendig	10
need, to	brauchen	4
new	neu	2, 4, 5
new (of a new type)	neuartig	10
next to	neben	7
Nice to meet you	Angenehm	1
no time	keine Zeit	3
noisy	laut	4
nose	Nase (f)	6

O

olive	Olive (f)	5
on (top), on (to)	auf	7
on business	beruflich	7
on, at	an	6, 7
open-plan office	Großraumbüro (n)	10
open, to	aufmachen	8
opera house	Opernhaus (n)	4
opposite	gegenüber	7
orange	Orange (f)	5
orange juice	Orangensaft (m)	5
order, to	bestellen	5
organise, to	organisieren	8
over, across	über	7

P

pack	Packung (f)	5
page	Seite (f)	4
painter	Maler (m)	2
pancake	Pfannkuchen (m)	6
paradise	Paradies (n)	6
parents' evening	Elternabend (m)	6
park (inner city)	Stadtpark (m)	3
parking meter	Parkuhr (f)	4
parking space	Parkplatz (m)	4
pass, to (exams)	bestehen	10
passport	Paß (m)	10
patient	Patient (m)	7
pay, to	bezahlen	7
pea	Erbse (f)	5
peninsula	Halbinsel (f)	6
perfect	perfekt	6
pharmacy	Apotheke (f)	4

physical exercise	körperliche Bewegung	9
piano	Klavier (n)	9
picture	Bild (n)	2, 8
piece	Stück (n)	5
pizza restaurant	Pizzeria (f)	4
place	Ort (m)	6
plan, to	planen	8
play piano, to	Klavier spielen	2
play, to	spielen	1
pleasant	angenehm	1
Please repeat.	Noch einmal, bitte.	1
politician	Politiker (m)	2
pork fillet	Schweinefilet (n)	5
postbox	Briefkasten (m)	4
postage stamp	Briefmarke (f)	4
postcard	Postkarte (f)	4
potato	Kartoffel (f)	5
powder	Trockenpulver (n)	7
prawn	Krabbe (f)	5
prescribe, to	verordnen	7
prime minister	Premierminister (m)	2
printer	Drucker (m)	8
priority	Priorität (f)	9
private life	Privatleben (n)	9
profession	Beruf (m)	2
programmer	Programmierer (m)	2
project report	Projektbericht (m)	3
pub	Kneipe (f)	6

Q

qualification	Qualifikation (f)	10
queue	Schlange (f)	8

R

radio programme	Radiosendung (f)	9
raincoat	Regenmantel (m)	8
raspberry	Himbeere (f)	5
reach, to	erreichen	6
read, to	lesen	2
reading the paper	Zeitungslesen (n)	9
realistic	realistisch	9
reception	Empfang (m)	5
recipe	Rezept (n)	5
recover, to	erholen	9
red wine	Rotwein (m)	5
regional train	Regionalzug (m)	8
rent, to	mieten	6

research, to	recherchieren	6
revolutionary	revolutionär	10
rice	Reis (m)	5
rich	reich	8
risotto	Risotto (m)	5
river	Fluß (m)	6
road	Straße (f)	2, 4, 6
roast pork	Schweinebraten (m)	5
role	Rolle (f)	2, 6
rollerblade, to	inlineskaten	2
roof	Dach (n)	7
roofer	Dachdecker (m)	7
room	Zimmer (n)	4
room number	Zimmernummer (f)	7
row	Streit (m)	9
row, series	Reihe (f)	6
rump steak	Rumpsteak (n)	5
run, to	rennen	8

S

sailing boat	Segelboot (n)	10
salmon	Lachs (m)	5
Saturday	Samstag (m), Sonnabend (m)	3
sausages (fried)	Bratwurst (f)	5
scallop	Jakobsmuschel (f)	5
school	Schule (f)	2
sea	Meer (n)	6
search engine	Suchmaschine (f)	10
secretary	Sekretärin (f)	2
See you!	Tschüs!	1
self-test	Selbsttest (m)	9
self-employed	Selbständige (pl)	9
sell, to	verkaufen	4
senior manager	Führungskraft (f)	9
sentence	Satz (m)	5
shampoo	Haarwaschmittel (n)	5
she	sie	1
shop, to	einkaufen	2, 4
shoulder	Schulter (f)	6
side	Seite (f)	4
sight	Sehenswürdigkeit (f)	6
simple	einfach	10
since	seit	7
sleep	Schlaf (m)	9
sleeping pill	Schlaftablette (f)	7
slice	Scheibe (f)	5
slow	langsam	5
small farm worker's		

cottage	Kate (f)	8
small	klein	4
sofa	Sofa (n)	10
sore throat	Halsschmerzen (pl)	7
soup	Suppe (f)	5
sour	sauer	8
sow, to	nähen	8
spare time	Freizeit (f)	9
spare, relaxed hour	Mußestunde (f)	9
special offer	Schnupperangebot (n)	6
spectacular	spektakulär	6
spend the night, to	übernachten	7
square	Platz (m)	4
start, to	beginnen	2
station, stop	Haltestelle (f), Station (f)	4
stomach	Bauch (m)	6
stomach ache	Bauchschmerzen (pl)	7
strange	merkwürdig	6
strawberry jam	Erdbeermarmelade (f)	9
street	Straße (f)	2, 4, 6
strict	streng	10
study, to	studieren	8
suitcase	Koffer (m)	8
surf the Internet, to	Internetsurfen	1
surf, to	surfen	1, 10
surname	Familienname (m)	1
swim, to	schwimmen	1, 2

T

table (grid)	Tabelle (f)	9
table (furniture)	Tisch (m)	5
tablet	Tablette (f)	7
take, to	nehmen	4
teacher	Lehrer (m)	2
telephone conversation	Telefongespräch (n)	7
telephone number	Telefonnummer (f)	2
tennis	Tennis (n)	1
terrace	Reihenhaus (n)	9
theatre	Theater (n)	1

thick, big	dick	8
Thursday	Donnerstag (m)	3
ticket machine	Fahrscheinautomat (m)	4
time	Zeit (f)	9
time after work	Feierabend (m)	9
tin	Dose (f)	5
tired	müde	3
to	zu	7
today	heute	3
toothache	Zahnschmerzen (pl)	7
tour guide	Reisebegleiter (m)	10
tourist information	Touristeninformation (f)	4
train	Zug (m)	4, 5
training provider	Fortbildungsinstitut (m)	5
travel, to	verreisen	6
trip around the world	Weltreise (f)	10
trouser suit	Hosenanzug (m)	9
trout	Forelle (f)	5
trumpet	Trompete (f)	9
Tuesday	Dienstag (m)	3
tuition	Unterricht (m)	3
turnover	Umsatz (m)	9

U

under, underneath	unter	7
unfortunately	leider	4
university	Universität (f)	4
university course	Studium (n)	8
unknown	unbekannt	6
unrealistic	unrealistisch	9
user-friendly	bedienungsfreundlich	10

V

vanilla ice-cream	Vanilleeis (n)	5
vegetables	Gemüse (n)	5
video recorder	Videorekorder (m)	10
view	Anblick (m)	6
village	Ort (m)	6

virtual	virtuell	2
visit, to	besuchen, besichtigen	2, 4, 6
vocabulary	Vokabeln (pl)	10

W

waiter (male)	Kellner (m)	5
waitress	Kellnerin (f)	5
walk, to	wandern	6
wall	Wand (f)	7
washing powder	Waschmittel (n)	5
watch TV, to	fernsehen	2
weather	Wetter (n)	9
Wednesday	Mittwoch (m)	3
week	Woche (f)	2, 6
weekend	Wochenende (n)	7
went wrong	ist schief gegangen	7
wet	naß	7
wheat beer	Weizenbier (n)	5
white cabbage	Weißkohl (m)	5
white wine	Weißwein (m)	5
wife	Frau (f)	1, 2
window	Fenster (n)	5
wine	Wein (m)	5
with	mit	5, 7
woman	Frau (f)	1, 2
wonderful	wunderschön	10
woods	Wald (m)	6
work place	Arbeitsplatz (m)	10
work, to	arbeiten	2
worry	Sorge (f)	6, 9
write, to	schreiben	5

Y

year	Jahr (n)	2, 6
yoghurt	Joghurt (m)	5
you (polite)	Sie	1
young	jung	1
zoo	Zoo (m)	4